Peru with Bolivia

Peru with Bolivia
THE INCA EMPIRE

Text
Rainer Waterkamp

Photographs
Arne Nicolaisen

Contents

Looking pretty: Girl in Pisac.

One of the Uro Islands on Lake Titicaca.

The mysterious ruins of Machu Picchu.

The Basilica Cathedral of Arequipa on the Plaza de Armas.

Still active: Ollagüe Volcano (5,869 meters/ 19,250 feet).

In the Amazon region, boats are often the only means of transport.

A traditional weaving loom.

Huaraz at the foot of the Cordillera Blanca.

*Bowler hat and bundles of charm:
A flower seller in Puno on Lake
Titicaca (above). Not only flowers,
fruit and vegetables grow around
the lake; reeds grow in abundance
on its shallow shores, making it
an ideal place for fishing (right).*

> "Peru! There it was: vast, mysterious, gray-green, dirt poor, infinite, wealthy, ancient, reticent."

Mario Vargas Llosa

Apart from the capital, Lima, the **Pacific Coast** offers unexpected treasures: magnificent temples and pyramids build of clay, princely graves filled with gold and mysterious markings in the desert sands bear witness to ancient cultures.

Colonial jewels and a silver mountain, snow-capped volcanoes, sparkling lakes and a vast salt desert: the barren **Altiplano** of Bolivia has a number of surprises in store.

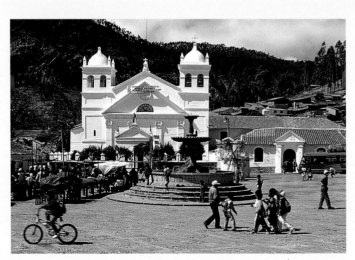

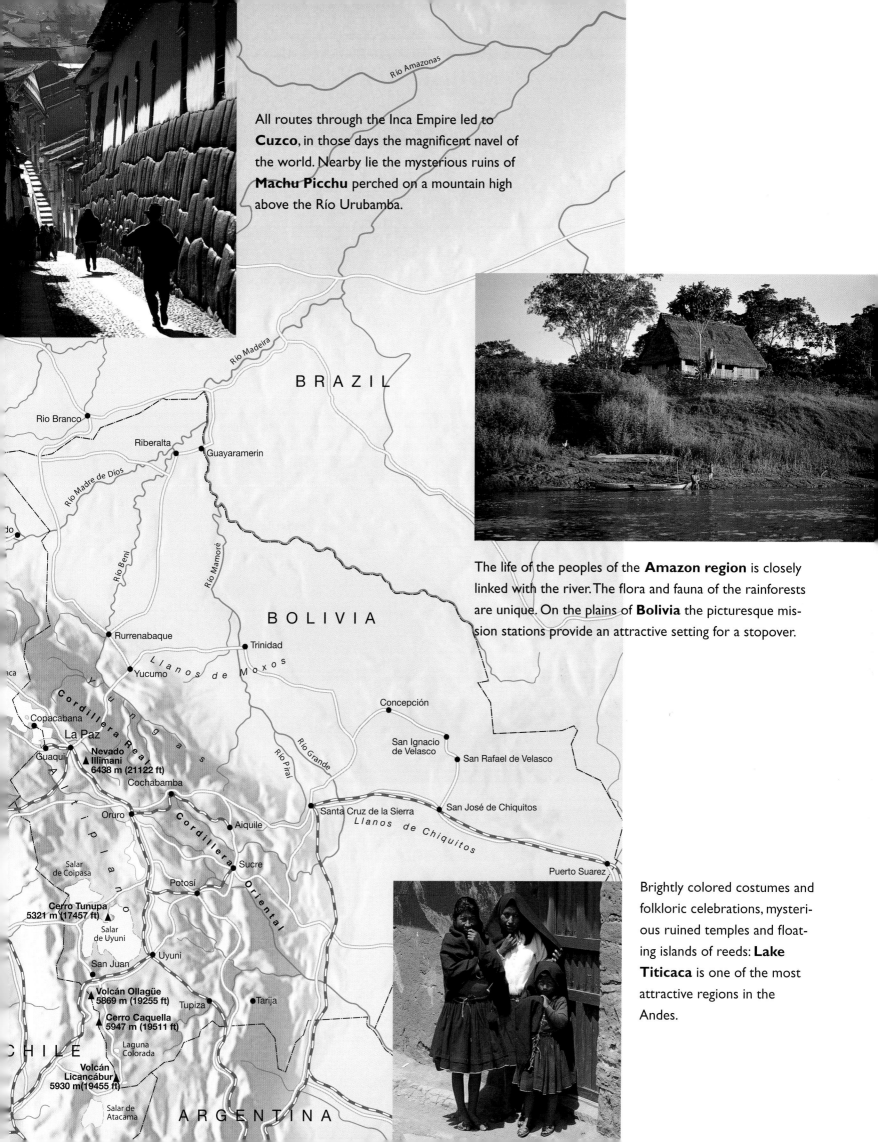

All routes through the Inca Empire led to
Cuzco, in those days the magnificent navel of
the world. Nearby lie the mysterious ruins of
Machu Picchu perched on a mountain high
above the Río Urubamba.

The life of the peoples of the **Amazon region** is closely
linked with the river. The flora and fauna of the rainforests
are unique. On the plains of **Bolivia** the picturesque mission stations provide an attractive setting for a stopover.

Brightly colored costumes and
folkloric celebrations, mysterious ruined temples and floating islands of reeds: **Lake
Titicaca** is one of the most
attractive regions in the
Andes.

Río Amazonas

Río Madeira

B R A Z I L

Rio Branco

Riberalta
Guayaramerin

Río Madre de Dios

Río Beni

Río Mamoré

B O L I V I A

Rurrenabaque

Trinidad

Llanos de Moxos

Yucumo

Cordillera Real

Copacabana

La Paz

Guaqui

Nevado
▲ Illimani
6438 m (21122 ft)

Cochabamba

Oruro

Aiquile

Cordillera Oriental

Altiplano

Salar
de Coipasa

Sucre

Potosí

Cerro Tunupa
5321 m (17457 ft) ▲

Salar
de Uyuni

San Juan

Uyuni

Volcán Ollagüe
▲ 5869 m (19255 ft)

Tupiza

Cerro Caquella
▲ 5947 m (19511 ft)

C H I L E

Laguna
Colorada

Volcán
Licancábur
5930 m (19455 ft)

Salar de
Atacama

A R G E N T I N A

Tarija

Río Pirai

Río Grande

Concepción

San Ignacio
de Velasco

San Rafael de Velasco

Santa Cruz de la Sierra

San José de Chiquitos

Llanos de Chiquitos

Puerto Suarez

In the Heart of the Inca Empire

Mountain peaks soaring heavenwards and the Pacific surf, tropical rain forests and deserts drier than the Sahara have created in Peru a series of unique landscapes full of contrasts. In 1558 the historian Pedro Cieza de León sent an enthusiastic report to King Philip II of Spain: "It is time to take up my pen and let the whole world know what I have to report about Peru." Yet an air of incomparable melancholy appears to lie across the country: the ruins of ancient cultures tell of a history steeped in blood and lived out on barren soil; of the will to survive and the struggles for freedom of the Indian peoples who were oppressed for centuries. And the country pays a high price for its natural beauty: Peru lies above the point where two of the Earth's mighty tectonic plates meet and rub against each other. At the so-called Peru-Chile Trench the Pacific Nazca Plate pushes across from the West underneath the South American continental plate. This results in massive pressure as rocky masses of vast size become interlocked and then break apart, often with a violent jolt, resulting in frequent and at times extremely violent earthquakes.

Over millions of years the pressure of the two plates produced the geological folding which created the Andes mountain chain, which runs like a spine down the entire length of the South American subcontinent stretching thousands of kilometers and miles from the Caribbean to Cape Horn. At the same time, magma forced its way through cracks in the rocks from the Earth's core to the surface, creating the 7,000-meter-high (23,000-foot) volcanoes, which can be seen from afar at regular intervals along the entire length of the Cordillera.

Traveling in Peru

Visitors with sufficient time at hand wishing to explore the country aside from the popular tourist haunts, and especially those prepared to accept a little discomfort now and then, will have an unforgettable experience in Peru – regardless of whether they

A land between wealth and poverty: Precious gold relics date from Peru's pre-Columbian past, like the Inca figurine of a Sun virgin wrapped in a manta (above). – This Indígena girl goes from door to door in the Andes village Chavín de Huántar, selling ribbons and herbs to supplement the family's meager income (right).

join a travel group or are adventurous enough to set off independently; whether they want to enjoy the landscape or explore ancient cultures; whether they are traveling in a jeep or by air on the longer sections of their trip – or even whether they are traveling as the locals do, by Indio train.

Nature lovers and mountaineers will find a "Peruvian Switzerland" in the Callejón de Huaylas, an impressive chain of lofty, snow-capped mountains which are among the highest in the country. The picturesque landscape of the verdant high valley between the Cordillera Blanca and the Cordillera Negra in the

In the Andes the people live as their ancestors from farming and cattle breeding (right). The field terraces in the Cañón del Colca, girdled by stone walls, are of the Inca period. In those days kiwicha and other cereals were grown (above).

abroad. In the meantime the government of Peru has changed its policies and now encourages the farming of old Indian crops because they are better adapted to local conditions than imported species. For example, kiwicha has been rediscovered – a type of cereal rich in protein, minerals and trace elements. Another feature of the government program is the reactivation of pre-Columbian terraced fields to be farmed again by traditional methods, thus permitting an optimal use of the land area. Research is also being carried out into traditional Indian medicine and its herbal remedies.

The Heritage of Ancient Cultures

Virtually fifty percent of all Peruvians are descendants of the original Indian population. Most of them live in the Andes highlands, a region which has preserved its original character to this day. The people there speak Quechua, the language of the Inca, or Aymará, which is current in the region surrounding Lake Titicaca. A further quarter of a million Indians of varying descent live in the Amazon lowlands. Then there are the mestizos, of mixed European/ Indian race, who make up one-third of the total population. In South America, only neighboring Bolivia can claim a

North of Peru makes it a paradise for trekking enthusiasts and mountaineers from all the corners of the globe.

But also the awe-inspiring emptiness of the Puna will enchant the visitor. On the railroad journey through the Andes highlands between Puno and Cuzco you will see the terraced fields of the Inca clinging to the steep mountain slopes. Many terraces are desolate and lie fallow – over the centuries, the ancient, productive farming methods of the Inca were sadly forgotten. Until a few years ago staple foods like rice, potatoes, corn and wheat, which were previously grown here, even had to be imported from

similarly high percentage of Indígenas – which is the Indios correct appellation.

It is not widely known that some two thousand years ago Peru was the site of a variety of cultures, some of which were highly developed. Numbering amongst them were the Moche (also known as the Mochica) and the Chimú, the Paracas and the Nazca, all of whom settled near the coast. Many treasures of these early civilizations have remained in a remarkably well-preserved state due to the dry climate. Especially famous are the ruins of Chan Chan in the North and the Valley of Pyramids near Túcume. The burial site of the Prince of Sipán is also worth visiting. For decades scientists have made countless attempts to decipher the meaning of the mysterious geoglyphs known as the Nazca Lines.

Visitors who wish to study the numerous pieces of evidence relating to pre-Columbian history and past events in Peru in more detail should go to the museums, especially those in the capital city of Lima. The National Museum of Archeology boasts more than 85,000 exhibits, the fascinating Museum of Gold on the out-

16

skirts of the city, houses an overwhelming number of gold exhibits found over the years as well as an impressive weapons collection and the Rafael Larco Herrera Museum features a valuable collection of ceramics from the pre-Inca period.

The Decline of the Inca

As the representatives of the last civilization of Pan-American significance, the Inca can be seen as the zenith of a series of highly

Reliefs carved into the clay, of dragons, rainbows, fish and other motifs decorate the walls of the Huaca del Dragón, a pyramid near Trujillo built during the 13th century by the Chimú.

developed cultures, which had preceded them. The term Inca applied originally exclusively to their godlike rulers; only later did the name become currency for the entire people. The golden age of the Inca Empire began in the early 15th century and lasted for barely a century. The arrival of the Spanish conquistadors in South America, however, sealed the fate of the Incas.

In 1493, only shortly after Columbus discovered the Caribbean Islands, en route to what he thought would be India, Huayna Cápac became the eleventh King of the Incas and the ruler of a vast empire extending from what is now Ecuador to the Río Maule in central Chile. He succeeded in extending his empire northwards, establishing a second power center in Quito to add to the other Cuzco.

During Huayna Cápa's last years of rule the Spaniard Francisco Pizarro sailed along the coast of the Inca Empire on a number of voyages of discovery. In 1527 he landed at Tumbes in the densely settled Gulf of Guayaquil and sent the Greek Pedro de Candía and a small group of his companions ashore to learn more about the legendary gold and silver treasures of the Inca. The historian Bernabé Cobo tells us how the Inca ruler received the news

See page 26   17

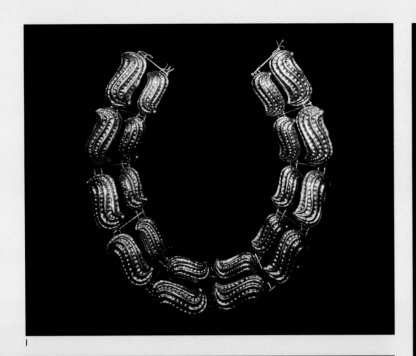

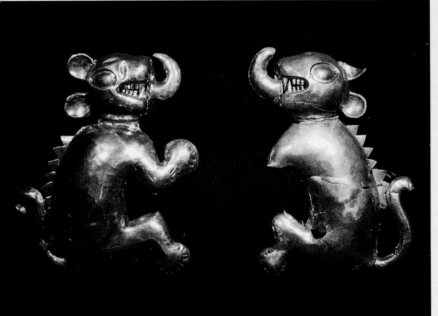

Archeological treasures from the
burial sites of pre-Inca cultures
were collected in the Museo
Arqueológico Nacional Brüning in
Lambayeque:
1 Chain of golden groundnuts;
2 Two golden dragon figures;
3 Gilt drinking vessel with representations of animals and men
(Ethnological Museum, Berlin);
4 Golden tunic with engravings.

5

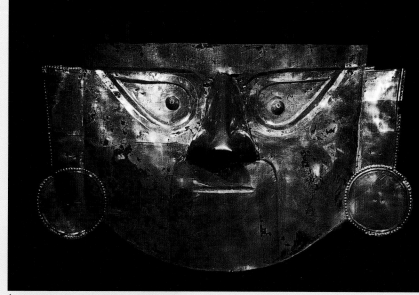

6

7

5 Among the grave objects found in North Peru were large earrings which nobles wore as a symbol of power in Inca times – here an example from Sicán with the figure of a mythical hero.

6 and 7 The earrings can also be clearly seen on the gold mask and on the little sculpture on the tumi, a ceremonial knife.

History in Dates and Pictures

1 17th-century Peruvian ship's peso showing the Pillars of Hercules. After being transported to Europe the silver coins were melted down. – 2 Túpac Amaru I, the last Inca ruler, was executed by the Spanish in 1572. – 3 A Spanish silver fleet sets sail (woodcut, around 1860). – 4 Contemporary portrait of the Spanish conquistador Francisco Pizarro (1476–1541). – 5 The Argentinian-born freedom fighter General José de San Martín (1778–1850; anonymous portrait c. 1850). 6 Portrait of the conquistador Hernando de Soto (1496–1542), who took part in Pizarro's conquest of Peru.

850 BC Construction of the temple fortress of Chavín de Huántar.

500 BC – 600 AD The golden age of pre-Inca cultures: Paracas, Recuay, Vircús, Cajamarca, Nazca and Moche.

c. 700 Expansion of the Tiahuanaco and Huari cultures.

c. 1200 Manco Cápac founds the Kingdom of the Inca.

1250 – 1460 Chimú Kingdom.

1438 – 1527 Inca power extends from Ecuador to Chile.

1492 Discovery of America.

1532 Francisco Pizarro begins his conquest of South America.

1533 The Spanish enter Cuzco, the Inca capital.

1536–1538 Inca revolt.

1541 Pizarro is assassinated.

1545 Rich silver deposits are discovered in Upper Peru (Bolivia).

1548 Execution of Gonzalo Pizarro; founding of La Paz in Bolivia.

1570 Introduction of the Inquisition.

1572 The Spanish conquer the last Inca province and execute Túpac Amaru, the son of Manco Cápac II, in Cuzco.

1650 A major earthquake destroys large parts of Cuzco.

1668 The Spanish found Puno

8

10

9

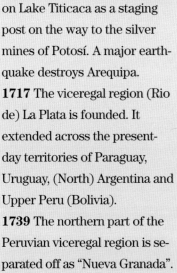

7

1983 Meteorological catastrophe in Peru and Ecuador; the El Niño current causes the flooding of 120,000 hectares (296,400 acres) of farmland.
1985 The government of socialist Alán García Perez comes to power; major economic crisis.
1990 Japanese-born President Alberto Kenya Fujimori takes office.
April 1992 Fujimori revokes constitution and dissolves Parliament.
September 1992 Arrest of Abimal Guzman, leader of the guerilla organization Sendero Luminoso
1996/1997 Japanese Embassy occupied by the Túpac Amaru terrorist group. Terrorists shot and hostages freed by the army.
November 2000 Fujimori resigns and flees to Japan.
July 2001 Alejandro Toledo is the first Indígena to become President of Peru.
June 2005 In Bolivia, President Carlos Mesa resigns following unrest. New interim president is Eduardo Rodriguez.
January 2006 Evo Morales is the first Indígena to become President of Bolivia.
2006 Following a runoff, Alan Garcia is again elected President in Peru, having previously held office from 1985 – 1990.
June – August 2007 Worst earthquake for 40 years in Peru; destruction in the Ica region (towns Pica, Ica, Chincha Alta) south of the capital Lima.

on Lake Titicaca as a staging post on the way to the silver mines of Potosí. A major earthquake destroys Arequipa.
1717 The viceregal region (Rio de) La Plata is founded. It extended across the present-day territories of Paraguay, Uruguay, (North) Argentina and Upper Peru (Bolivia).
1739 The northern part of the Peruvian viceregal region is separated off as "Nueva Granada".

7 Túpac Amaru II, the leader of the Indian revolt against the Spanish in 1780. – 8 Marriage of Don Martín Garcia Oñez de Loyola (St. Ignatius Loyola's nephew) to Doña Beatriz Clara Coya Ñusta (Sayri Túpac's daughter). – 9 The earthquake of August 16, 2007 also destroyed virtually all the houses in the village of Ica. – 10 The Peruvian earthquake in August 2007: Evo Morales, President of Bolivia, shows solidarity in a visit to Peru's President Alan Garcia (r.).

1746 A 20-meter high (66-feet) tidal wave reaches the coast of Peru and destroys Callao, the port of Lima.
1767 The Jesuits are expelled from the Spanish colonies.
1776 The southern part of the Peruvian viceregal region is separated off as the viceregal region of "La Plata".
1780–81 Revolts in Peru and Bolivia (Túpac Amaru II in Peru, Túpac Katari in Bolivia).
1809 Pedro Murillo declares the independence of Charcas province.
1812 Simón Bolívar takes over leadership in South America's struggle for liberation.
1820 José de San Martín lands with his troops in Peru.
1821 The provinces of Upper Peru and Lower Peru declare independence.
1825 Upper Peru declares its independence under the name "República de Bolivia".
1836 Bolivian troops under

President Andrés Santa Cruz win a campaign against Peru. The result is the (violent) formation of a union between the two countries.
1839 Chilean and Argentinian troops invade Peru and force the dissolution of the Peruvian-Bolivian Union.
1879 – 1883 The War of the Pacific (Saltpeter War) between Chile, Peru and Bolivia; Bolivia loses its access to the Pacific.
1929 Peace treaty with Chile. Peru forced to cede its two southernmost provinces, Arica and Tarapacá, to Chile.
1941/42 Border conflict with Ecuador in the Amazon region; Peru gains 200,000 sq. km. (77,200 sq. miles)
1943 – 85 In both Peru and Bolivia, military dictatorships alternate with democratically elected governments.
1967 Ché Guevara captured and shot in the Bolivian jungle

21

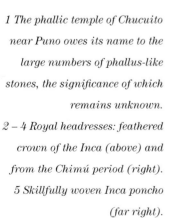

1 The phallic temple of Chucuito near Puno owes its name to the large numbers of phallus-like stones, the significance of which remains unknown.
2 – 4 Royal headresses: feathered crown of the Inca (above) and from the Chimú period (right).
5 Skillfully woven Inca poncho (far right).

22

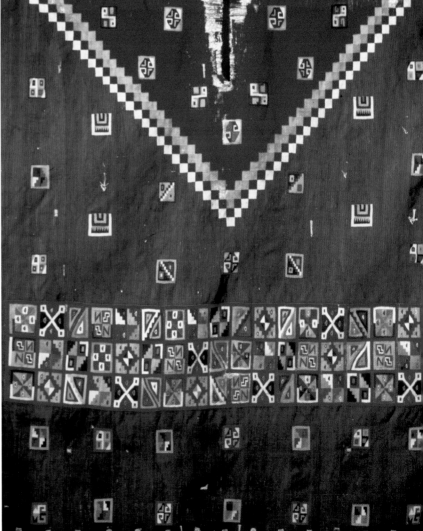

9

6

7

8

10

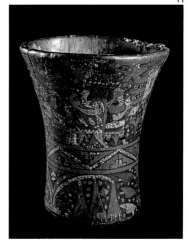

11

6–8, 10 and 11
The pre-Columbian cultures produced skillfully made ceramics
and vessels.
9 The temple complex of the Huaca
de la Luna was built around
500 AD by monks at the foot of the
Cerro Blanco south of Trujillo
(illustration).

23

In the Valle Sagrado, the "Sacred Valley" of the Inca.

of the Spanish landing: "Huayna Cápac was relaxing and feasting in his palaces in Tumibamba when runners brought him news from his governor in Tumbes. Breathless and alarmed at what had happened they reported to the Inca that strange foreigners such as had never been seen before had landed on the beach of Tumbes. Their faces were white and bearded and they wore clothes covering their entire bodies and generally looked very wild. The Inca king was speechless when he heard the news; he was so concerned that he was overcome with melancholy and shut himself in his private apartment, and did not re-appear until darkness fell."

According to the chronicler Pedro Sarmiento de Gamboa (1532–1592) the dying Inca proclaimed Ninán Cuyuchi as his heir (who would die soon like his predecessor of the plague) and, failing him, Huáscar, who was still in Cuzco. Atahualpa accompanied his father's body to Tumibamba with the well-trained army, which he left in Quito. At the same time, in Cuzco, Huáscar was attempting to

26

Threatening dark clouds gather above a high plain in the Cordillera Blanca, whose snow-capped summits are among the highest in Peru (above). The mountainous region is also known as "Peruvian Switzerland" because of the beauty of the landscape (above right). – Sheep and cattle are the farmers' most valuable possessions in the Andes (left).

secure his position as Inca ruler with his sister, Chuqui Uzpai. Huayna Cápac did not live to see the fall of his empire. It is not certain exactly in which year the last great Inca ruler died, although many experts put it at 1527. His demise was caused by one of the diseases the Spanish introduced to the New World on their military campaigns, which were to claim the lives of many hundreds of thousands of the continent's original inhabitants.

After the death of Huayna Cápac an embittered quarrel for succession broke out between the Inca ruler's sons Atahualpa and Huáscar, plunging the empire into bloody civil war. Under these circumstances it is not surprising how easy it was for Francisco Pizarro to overturn and plunder the largest and most powerful empire in South America with a force of 183 men and 37 horses. In 1532 Charles V of Spain proclaimed him Royal Governor and Captain General of the Inca Empire that was about to be conquered.

For the Indígenas, daily life has scarcely changed over the past centuries. To this day they have to travel long distances on foot to get to the market, as here on the Altiplano by Lake Titicaca.

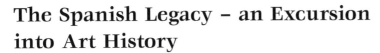

The Spanish Legacy – an Excursion into Art History

Lifestyle on the Pacific Coast and in the larger cities such as Lima, Arequipa and Trujillo is unmistakably Spanish in style. The Creoles, as the descendants of the Spanish born in Peru are known, have largely preserved the customs of their ancestors and endowed the colonial cities with a European atmosphere. This can be seen not least in the numerous churches and monasteries as well as in a variety of other buildings.

Two periods can be distinguished in the development of colonial art and architecture. From 1550 until 1700 the Indian world was progressively subjected to Hispanic influences; the most characteristic elements are the Plateresque and Churrigueresque

styles. Between 1700 and 1780 a synthesis of Christian-Iberian and indigenous motifs took place to be witnessed most significantly in the works of the Cuzco School (see page 76).

The Plateresque style incorporated elements from the Moorish tradition, especially the lavish use of arabesques. The Churrigueresque style was named after the Spanish sculptor and builder José Churriguera (1650–1724), who introduced an exuberant Baroque style into the churches. Yet another style, the

Mudéjar style, is a synthesis of Romanesque, Gothic and Arabian architectural elements.

Around 1690 another style developed which came to be known as Mestizo Baroque or Andine Baroque. Here motifs of Indígena mythology were mixed with European models. A century later it was replaced by neo-classical trends which established themselves by approximately 1850 emphasizing clarity of line and a strict sense of balance.

How Amerigo became America

The name "America" goes back to the German cartographer Martin Waldseemüller and the work he published in 1507, Cosmographia introductio, in which he suggested the name "America" for the newly discovered continent in the West.

On a world map he drew that year he labeled South America "America" (the name later became the term for the entire continent).

In so doing Waldseemüller paid tribute to the Florentine explorer Amerigo Vespucci, who from 1499 until 1504 sailed in the service of Spain and Portugal along the Atlantic coast of South America from Brazil as far as the estuary of the Río de la Plata and possibly even further.

It soon became clear that the continent he had discovered was not the Asia he had been searching for, but truly a "New World."

29

Lima – the New Center of Power

Although it is mostly desert, featuring little more than sand dunes and bare rocks and therefore one of the lesser hospitable regions of Peru, more than 70 percent of all Peruvians live on the coast. Some seven million people cram into the Lima metropolitan area alone – about one third of the total population.

Life here is determined by religious belief: Mass in San Miguel de Velasco, and blessing a new car in Copacabana ...

Peru's capital was founded on the Feast of the Epiphany in 1535 by Francisco Pizarro. Soon after, the *Ciudad de los Reyes* the "City of the Kings" became the arena for violent power struggles. This time, however, the Spanish conquistadors were pointing their swords at their own countrymen. In the argument as to how the conquered territory should be divided up after the defeat of the Incas, in 1538 Francisco Pizarro had his former comrade-in-arms Diego de Almagro executed. Three years later Pizarro

... or at the "Snow Stars Festival" on the Nevado Auzangate, in which the pilgrims carry crosses up onto a glacier during a procession at night. Like the Cathedral in Lima, many churches are elaborately decorated with gold ornamentation (above).

31

was assassinated in his palace in Lima by supporters of Diego de Almagros. His fate was described thus by chronicler Augustin de Zárate: "Finally he fell, struck with a deadly dagger wound in the throat. As he fell he cried out loudly for the Last Sacrament, and when he could no longer speak, he made the sign of the cross on the ground with his hand and kissed it. And so he recommended his soul to God." Fighting between the conquistadors continued.

In 1543, King Charles V proclaimed Lima headquarters of the Spanish vice-regal possessions in Peru, which extended across the whole of South America with the exception of Brazil. The first viceroy, Blasco Nuñez Vela, arrived in Peru in 1544, but the conquistadors in the entourage of Gonzalo Pizarro, a brother of Francisco, feared for their sinecures and joined in a conspiracy against the crown representatives. Nuñez Vela died in 1546 fight-

ing against Gonzalo's army. In the four years, from 1544 until 1548, Gonzalo Pizarro was able to enjoy his vast power ruling over a Peru that spread from Quito as far as Chile and Argentina. Based, as it was, on terror, and revenues from the newly discovered silver mines in Potosí backed by his command of a 23-ship armada, Pizarro's rule seemed invincible.

It was the King's emissary Pedro de la Gasca who finally succeeded in conquering Gonzalo Pizarro on the plain of Jaquijahuana near Cuzco. Even before battle commenced, Gonzalo's closest companions deserted him, taking a large number of troops and joined forces under de la Gasca's command. Pizarro was executed on April 10, 1548, thereby almost becoming a martyr. But after de la Gasca left, revolt and private feuds between the conquistadors flared up once more. The search for gold and glory continued, but El Dorado, the legendary "Land of Gold", was never found.

In the Cerro Rico, the "Silver Mountain" of Potosí, ore mining still goes on (above). The silver was used to make vast quantities of coins in the municipal mint (right). Evidence of wealth can also be seen in the rooms of the Casa Dorada in Tarija, built by a merchant in 1930 (center). Llama path in the Andes east of Cuzco (main photo).

The Government of the New World

Peru under the viceroy was divided into Audiencias (judicial regions), whose courts (also called audiencias) were intended to counter attempts at independence and the arbitrary dealings of the conquistadors. The Audiencias were the extended arm of the central Spanish government and as such they carried out judicial

and legislative as well as administrative duties. They could appeal directly to the Indian Council in Madrid (Consejo Real y Supremo de las Indias), founded in 1524. It was directly responsible to the Crown and had overall control over Spain's overseas possessions.

One of the wealthiest regions in Peru was the Audiencia de Charcas, which extended across the Altiplano of Bolivia, Paraguay and the regions around the Río de la Plata. Not far from the provincial capital of La Plata, present-day Sucre in Bolivia, near Potosí, lay the Cerro Rico. This mountain was discovered

for its plentiful silver in 1545 and for more than 200 years provided the basis for the fame and power of the Spanish Empire. Power games at the expense of several million Indígenas and African slaves who were worked to death in the silver mines.

Poverty and Oppression

Throughout Peru the Indígenas were compelled into forced labor (mita). Although an edict of King Philip II of 1576 proclaimed the bondage or feudal system (*encomienda*) as "one of the rights of

34

See page 38

The Sunday market at Pisac offers a wide variety of potatoes, onions, corn and other vegetables and a great variety of craftworks and utensils for everyday needs (left).

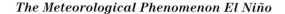

Even the small boys wear the traditional men's clothing of the Andean Highlands: the chullu with ear flaps and the poncho (above right). The girls dress like their mothers in a woollen shawl, knitted jacket and brightly-colored knee-length skirts, of which they wear several, one on top of the other (left).

The Meteorological Phenomenon El Niño

The trade winds normally blow westwards, driving the warm water on the surface of the Pacific from America towards Southeast Asia, where they build up. Warm, damp air masses gather above the warm ocean and then fall as monsoon rain. The air flows back at high altitude and sinks down again above the East Pacific. There is usually no rainfall here.

In El-Niño years there is little difference in air pressure between the Eastern and Western Pacific. The trade winds die down, the warm water flows back eastwards and forces back the cold water. The clouds which normally bring fall rainfall to Indonesia and Australia reach South America which results in heavy rainfall.

In the Land of the Potato

The Cuisine of Peru and Bolivia

2

1

3

4

1, 2, 4 and 5 In the market at Yungay, fruit and vegetables, live piglets and freshly plucked chickens are on sale. You can try Andean delicacies right next to the stalls.

3 In Lima you can even buy a whole roast pig, prepared on the spot with onions, salad and bread.

6 and 7 Fiery red chili pods are to be found everywhere in Peru, along with white beans and long sweet potatoes. – 8 A specialty of the coastal regions: fish with yucca fruits, plantains and limes.

9 Anticuchos, marinated ox heart, is cooked on a spit on a charcoal grill and served with potatoes.

Peru's cuisine is as varied as the geography and culture of the country. As Peru is the actual home of the potato, there are many different ways of preparing the tuber here.

Papa a la Huancaina, features boiled potatoes cut into thin slices and served with a chili and cheese sauce while *Papa ocapa* has them covered with a hot groundnut sauce. Both hors d'oeuvres are garnished with hard-boiled eggs and olives.

A typical dish in the Andes is *chairo*, a meat soup with *chuño* (black potatoes, freeze-

36

dried in the icy mountain climate), and *choclo*, a chicken dish with corn on the cob or *fritanga*; pork in pepper sauce with mint. Cuy picante, grilled guinea pig, is a great specialty in the Andes regions. *Pachamanca* is a tasty mixture of

meat and vegetables cooked on heated stones in a hole in the ground.

If you like roast pork with garlic and pepper, you should order *lechón*. *Lechón al horno* is barbecued suckling pig with

sweet potatoes and plantains. If you order *chicharrones*, the waiter will bring you roast pork crackling.

In Peru steaks are called *lomo*, *churrasco* or even *bistek*. *Lomo montado* is a beef steak served with two eggs, rice and fried banana. *Picante de pollo* or *picante mixto* is chicken fried in egg and groundnut flour; it

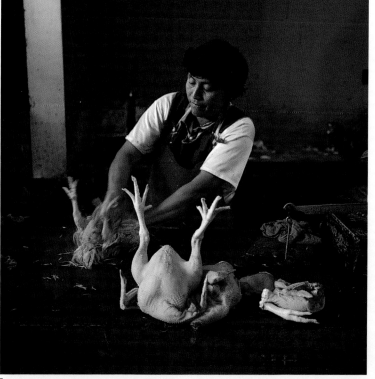

5

6   7

8   9

is served with fried potatoes, rice and salad with chilli. Rice and potatoes are also served with *mechado de cordero*, leg of lamb.

Anticuchos is a great specialty along the coast of Peru. It is marinated ox heart, cooked on a spit above a charcoal fire and seasoned with *aji*, hot chili. Naturally, fish dishes

dominate areas around the coastline such as *ceviche de corvina*: fresh sea bass, cut into small pieces and marinated for several hours before serving in lemon and orange juice.

In the Amazon jungle – as well as in the expensive restaurants in Lima – grilled tapir meat, *sachavaca*, cooked over an open fire or a charcoal grill, is a popular dish. The Amazon is rich in fish and provides the ingredients for *picadillos de paiche:* chopped and cooked *paiche* fish with tomatoes, eggs, onions, garlic, pepper and potatoes.

If you visit Bolivia you can sample *marraqueta*, a delicious bread, and *fricassee*, a spicy pork stew, in the restaurants of La Paz. The specialties of Sucre are *chorizos*, spicy pork sausages with onions and garlic, and *fricas*, chopped pork with maize beans and Chuño potatoes.

Many menus in Bolivia offer *chupe*, a clear meat and vegetable soup, *parillada*, grilled pork and beef steak with salad and potatoes. *Saltena* is is a bread-like pie filled with meat, vegetables, eggs, potatoes, a hot sauce and chili.

After the main course the Peruvians indulge their sweet tooth with desserts such as *picarones*; fried cake filled with cream and sprinkled with sugar.

37

the servants of the Crown through the grace of God, throughout their entire life and that of their heirs to receive tribute from the Indios and to be responsible for their material and spiritual welfare," the encomenderos carried out their responsibilities conscientiously only with regard to their demands for tribute; their duties were woefully neglected when they referred to the welfare of those under their protection.

The chronicler Felipe Huamán Poma de Ayala *(see page 66 f.)*, son of an Inca princess and a Spaniard, attacked the outrageous

exploitation in his 1,200-page work *El primer nueva crónica y buen gobierno*: "The Indios are forced to work as farm laborers and stable boys, as gardeners, shepherds and beasts of burden. The wives of the encomenderos are even worse than their husbands. The encomenderos compel the natives to exchange their cattle for wine. They force them to make ribbons, cloth and clothing, do not allow them to return home by day or by night and pay them no wages." The corregidores, who were appointed by the Crown to supervise the activities of the encomenderos, were often even more unscrupulous. The conditions of the miners in Potosí were equally inhuman. The temperatures in the underground tunnels often reached 50 °C (122 °F); the Indígenas mostly worked in groups of three in shifts of five days and five nights, during which time they were not permitted to leave the mine.

In a report dated May 4, 1718 the Indian Council recommended to King Philip V of Spain: "For the sake of your Royal conscience the Indian Council sees itself compelled to draw Your Majesty's attention to the fact that it can neither be justified by conscience nor by law that the mines should continue to be operated with the assistance of Mita Indians." A year later the King signed a law abolishing the work of the Mita in the mines of Potosí, but it was never put into operation – Philip V later retracted it.

The Plaza Mayor with its magnificent cathedral marks the historic center of Lima. It is a popular place for a stroll (left). The glass tower of the Banco Nuevo in Miraflores is the landmark of the new Lima (above). The ancient, brightly painted buses, originally from the U.S., are a feature of the cityscape (below).

In the vicinity of what is now Paraguay a number of independent Jesuit missions, so-called reductions, sprang up during the 18th century, where the Indígenas could live in freedom from the bondage of the conquistadors, provided they converted to the Christian faith. But at times they were not even safe from the "Holy Pursuit" (*cazas sagradas*) of the slave hunters, since the reductions were a thorn in the side of many a clerical and worldly dignitary. On April 2, 1767 King Charles III decreed that all reductions in

the years. Among Pizarro's companions was a missionary priest, Fray Vicente de Valverde, who played an important role in the capture and subsequent execution of the Inca ruler Atahualpa. A few years later Valverde was appointed the first Bishop of Cuzco by Pope Paul III: it was the first bishopric on South American soil.

Eye-witness accounts tell us how the representatives of the Catholic Church were not only interested in converting the original inhabitants but also in the plunder of Inca treasures. Magnifi-

South America should be dissolved, and the Jesuits were expelled.

By 1792, only 600,000 Indígenas remained of the population of many millions in Peru that had once lived under Huayna Cápac. Many thousands had succumbed to the disease which the conquistadors had introduced, but the majority of those original inhabitants were victim to the cruelty of the Spanish colonial rule – genocide in the Crown's name with the Church's blessing.

On a Papal Mission

The strong influence of the Catholic Church in Peru is in evidence to this day, although it has undergone a number of changes over

On the Inca Trail, which runs at altitudes between 2,200 and 4,200 meters (7,216 – 13,776 feet), you can see blossoming cactuses.

In the footprints of the Inca: the suspension bridge near Huichiri is made of plaited straw and is renewed every two years (left-hand page). – The Inca Trail leads across stony paths from Cuzco to Machu Picchu (above).

The Cordillera Blanca in Northern Peru is a paradise for mountaineers from all the corners of the globe; only the Asian Himalayas can offer more 6,000-meter (20,000-feet) peaks. The steep, craggy Alpamayo (5,947 meters/ 19,506 feet) is regarded as one of the most beautiful peaks in the world (right-hand page).

cant Churches stand today as testament to the prosperity behind the energetic building activities of those Christian missionaries.

Only a handful did otherwise, such as the Dominican priest Don Bartolomé de las Casas, who acted as spokesman on behalf of the rights of the Indígenas. In 1542 he protested to King Charles V of Spain against the inhuman treatment of the native Indians suggesting African slaves as stronger and more capable to replace them. To prevent the Indians from becoming extinct it was necessary to introduce slavery. Of course de las Casas was simply replacing one evil with another: the slave trade introduced as a consequence drove millions of Africans to misery and death.

Some four centuries later, South America became the birthplace of the "Theology of Liberation", whose purpose is to represent the poor and oppressed. Among the "Fathers" of this popular religious approach, which gained significant ground during the 1970s, was the priest Gustavo Gutierrez, born, 1928 in Peru, who has spent the past years working with the inhabitants of the slums of Lima.

Peruvian Reminiscences

You need to be very fit to be able to climb Mount Huascarán, the highest mountain in Peru (6,768 meters/ 22,199 feet). On a mountain ridge behind the base camp the summit of Huascarán Norte soars upward (6,655 meters/ 21,834 feet) (above).

The memories one returns with from a journey to Peru and Bolivia are as varied as the land itself: memories of surprising discoveries, unforgettable encounters and dangers one has survived, as well as disappointments, privations and the human suffering of the Indígenas, who have lived in very primitive conditions for centuries. They are memories of breathtakingly beautiful natural landscapes, such as the mountains of the Cordillera Blanca with its majestic summits; the fascinating variety of the flora and fauna of the Amazon rain forest; or the crystal-clear air of Lake Titicaca. In some places Nature is terrifyingly merciless, as in the coastal deserts or in the icy caves of the Andean Highlands, which are clothed in a unique silence, at times giving way to an endless melancholy. In spite of all the social, economic and political problems Peru is beset by, it is a country well worth discovering.

Viewed from the West it becomes clear why the Alpamayo is also known as the "Peruvian Matterhorn" (above). Nearby towers the imposing Huandoy Massif (right).

On the summit of the Nevado Ishinca.

Myths, Festivals and Ruined Cities

The Civilization around Lake Titicaca

The inhabitants of Isla Taquile in Lake Titicaca are famous for their festive hats (above), weaving (right-hand page) and brightly colored knitting (right). The natives call the reeds totora; they are used by the Uros to weave their boats (center).

The deep blue lake, the name of which is derived from the Aymará word *titi* (puma) and the Quechua expression *kaka* (rock), is up to 300 meters (984 feet) deep. Its location at 3,810 meters (12,497 feet) above sea level makes it one of the highest navigable lakes in the world. The surface of the vast inland expanse of water covers 8,300 square kilometers (3,204 square miles). It stores warmth, producing a mild climate along its shores. Here, and on the lake islands, live the descendants of the Uros, who once called themselves "Lake People." Not even the Incas succeeded in conquering this proud people, who avoided having to pay tribute by retreating into the impenetrable thicket of reeds surrounding Lake Titicaca. Today there are no more true Uros, since they have intermarried with the Aymará over the centuries and have also adopted the language of the latter. And yet, the Uros of Lake Titicaca are regarded as the Indígenas with the strongest tradition in the entire country.

Puno – The Capital of Folklore

Puno is one of the largest towns on Lake Titicaca. After rich silver deposits were found near Laikakota in 1657 a settlement grew up here and expanded rapidly. In 1668 it was formally founded by the Viceroy as *Villa Ricca de San Carlos de Puno*.

Today Puno is regarded as the folklore capital of Peru. A succession of folk festivals fills the annual calendar, whereby the most colorful are without doubt the Fiesta de la Virgen de la Can-

This is where it all began: according to legend, the Isla del Sol on the Bolivian side of Lake Titicaca (in the foreground) is the birthplace of the Inca dynasty.

delaria on February 2 (Candlemas) and the Puno Week in November, recalling the legendary arrival of the first Inca Manco Cápac and his sister-consort Mama Ocllo from the lake. The high point of the festivities of the Fiesta de la Virgen de la Candelaria is the Diablada, the "Festival of the Masked Devils"; it lasts for several days, during which the dancers cavort through the narrow alleys of Puno with the various groups competing with each other. They are accompanied by the "Devil's Band", which loudly supports the diablada rhythm.

Mysterious Burial Towers

In the icy-clear air of Sillustani the wind blows sharp, cold and full of sand. The endless expanses of the Puna, the Andean Highlands, extend as far as the eye can see. At almost 4,000 meters (13,120 feet) above sea level, only hard grass, cactuses and thorn bushes thrive. Ichú, a tough, prickly, brown-green grass, provides the basic foodstuff for the herds of llamas and alpacas living here.

This lonely setting is dotted with isolated farmhouses, their roofs thatched with straw and reeds. The air is incredibly clear; low clouds and dense, suddenly parting curtains of rain provide an impressive natural spectacle above the lonely countryside.

On a 150-meter (492-foot) high mountain on a peninsula on the Laguna de Umayo south of Sillustani stand circular and rec-

The reeds which grow along the shores of Lake Titicaca are a popular building material (above). The Uros use it not only for their huts and their boats, but even to construct floating islands.
Indígena women seldom leave the house without a hat. The shape and color reveal where they come from (below).

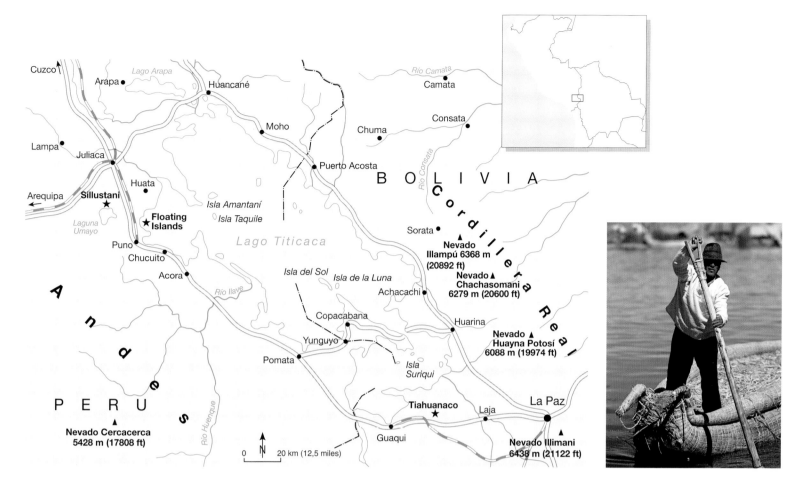

tangular burial towers known as chullpas, constructed of carefully worked basalt and trachyte stones which have been assembled without the use of mortar. Between 1200 and 1450 the region featured noble burial grounds of the Colla culture the Incas conquered it. The largest burial tower, the Chullpa del Lagarto, is 12 meters (39 feet) high. It extends vertically to over five stories and is topped by a dome. The entrances to the burial chambers were very low and faced East.

The thin air on the climb up to the Chullpas makes it hard going, but the mint growing between the grass provides welcome relief.

Life in the Reeds

A boat trip from Puno to the "floating islands" of the Uros is one of the highlights of a visit to Lake Titicaca. After first arriving in water taxi you can relax and be transported in style around the islands in a reed boat.

Reflections in the dark blue of the vast lake, with 8,300 square kilometers (3,200 square miles) the second largest lake of South America, make distances here deceptive and difficult to judge. Water birds hunt for food in the well stocked waters. Apart from the quiet sound of the boat's engine there is complete silence. Around the islands the water is clear and shallow and the lake bed easily visible.

The Uros propel their reed boats through the flat waters along the shore of the lake with poles or paddles (above). – Tiny Andean villages are dotted around Lake Titicaca, the simple houses usually congregate around a pretty colonial church (below).

53

The broad expanses of rushes look more like fields. They provide the fundaments for almost everything the Uros require for everyday life: boats, huts, and the islands themselves are formed of countless layers of reeds. It takes between six to twelve months for the reeds which make up the boats and the islands to become waterlogged and begin to rot so they have to be renewed regularly.

The Temple City of Tiahuanaco

Beyond the made-up road linking La Paz with Lake Titicaca lies the ruined temple complex of Tiahuanaco. It represents the historical zenith of Pre-Columbian Bolivia. A thousand years on and still the reason for the decline of this magnificent culture, whose golden age dated from 600 – 1000 AD, is unknown.

On the mainland (left-hand page, below) and on the islands of Amantaní (large photo) and Taquile (left), as well as fishing in the lake, the people breed sheep and grow potatoes, beans and cereals for food. Anything not needed to feed the family is sold on the market at Puno, the largest town on Lake Titicaca (below).

The remains of the Tiahuanaco culture are scattered across a wide area the precise extent of which, to this day, has not been fully determined. Over the centuries, unfortunately, the ruined city served as a stone quarry, most recently for the construction of the railroad line from La Paz to Guaqui at the southern tip of Lake Titicaca. It is hard to imagine that there was once a city here in which several tens of thousands of people lived and worked.

What remained after the Spanish plundering, the reuse of the stones for building materials and what was smuggled out by foreign archeologists is still very impressive. We have the Austrian engineer Arthur Posnansky, who made the investigation of Tiahuanaco his life's work, to thank for photographs of structures which were then blown up only a few hours after he had taken them. The images he recorded form a valuable foundation for restoration work.

Archeologists divide the ruins of Tiahuanaco into three main sections: Kalasasaya, Acapana and Pumapuncu. At 15 meters high, 180 meters long and 140 meters wide (49.2 x 590 x 459 feet) the Acapana Pyramid is one of the greatest puzzles within the ruined city. Scientists cannot tell whether it was used as a fortification, a sacrificial building or a temple.

Nearby stands a semi-subterranean temple, set some two meters (6.5 feet) into the ground. This is Templete Semisubterráneo, excavated in 1960 by Bolivian archaeologist Carlos Ponce Sanginés. Protruding from the red sandstone walls forming a rectangle 26 x 28 meters (85 x 92 feet) are the heads of well-preserved nails of limestone and tuff. A staircase leads down into the temple with three steles; No. 15 (Monolito Barbado), representing a deity with nose ornaments, is over two-and-a-half meters (8 feet) high.

55

It was in this temple, in 1934, that archeologist Wendell Bennett discovered the seven-meter high (23 feet) Pachamama Stele which bears his name (Monolito Bennett), whereupon it was exhibited in the Tiahuanaco Open-Air Museum in La Paz until 68 years later, in March 2002, it was returned to Tiahuanaco.

Another staircase leads from the Templete Semisubterráneo through the East Gate to Kalasasaya Temple, the best-reconstructed section of Tiahuanaco. It stands on a three-meter (10-foot) platform and is thought to date from the fifth century AD. It

consists of a massive rectangle with a base of 128 by 118 meters (420 x 387 feet). Its name goes back to the Aymará word for "Standing Stones" and refers to the monolithic sculptures found here.

Intipuncu, the "Sun Gate", is also a part of the Kalasasaya complex. One of the most famous monuments in the Andes it was carved from a single massive block of andesite. The bas-relief on the cross section is especially interesting: at the centre the figure of a "weeping god" is feature with a disproportionately large head and halo, out of which tiny puma heads appear to leap out. The figure, also known as *Dios de baculos* ("the god of the rods") holds in both hands a scepter with condor heads. It is probably a predecessor of Viracocha, who later became celebrated throughout the entire Andes region as the god of heaven and creation.

The god holding the scepter is usually portrayed standing on a stepped platform facing the front, both hands holding rods or similar objects of symbolic import. Aside from Tiahuanaco he is also to be found in regions influenced by the Pucará and Huari cultures. The god's mask-like face, framed by the rays of a halo-like headdress, clothed in a sort of tunic with a belt and skirt is typical. The figure is often accompanied by winged human-like figures. Decapitated human heads are another important motif. The Tiahuanaco and Huari may have been inspired by older art forms in order to demonstrate continuity and awareness of tradition.

Through the Sun Gate visitors have a magnificent view of the Ponce, a tall monolith named for the archaeologist Ponce Sanginés. Artistically created reliefs are a feature here too. To this day the numerous signs, featuring countless angular spirals, have yet to be deciphered. In another corner, the weathered red sandstone

monolith El Fraile ("The Monk") stands. The outstanding feature of this monument is the representation of crabs around its middle.

About one kilometer south is a third archeological site: what remains of the temple pyramid Pumapuncu, are vast stone blocks, each weighing some 130 tons. It is considered that some of the stones are actually harbor remains as the water level of Lake Titicaca would have been around 15 meters (49 feet) higher than today, thus the reaches of the lake would have been far greater.

The Sacred Islands of the Inca

Less than 100 kilometres (62.5 miles) north of Tiahuanaco in Lake Titicaca is the Isla del Sol (Sun Island) and Isla de la Luna (Moon Island). Long before you arrive you can see the islands and rocks, rising above the waters of the lake in Bolivian territory.

Heavily laden: mules are an ideal means of transport for reeds (left-hand page), which the inhabitants of Lake Titicaca use as building material for their huts and houses. The reeds' remarkable capacity for load-bearing is evidenced by the huts on the floating islands belonging to the Uros (above). – Among the everyday items of clothing worn by the women on the Isla Taquile is a woolen cloth they use to cover their heads (bottom left).

see page 62

View from the Isla Taquile to the Cordillera Real.

Sons of the Sun

On the Origins of the Inca Dynasty

1 A dancer at the Inti Raymi festival, which is celebrated in the inca ruins of Sacsayhuamán to mark the winter solstice.
2 The founder of the Inca dnasty, Manco Cápac ("Oil on Wood").

3 The most important deity in the Inca kingdom was Inti, the god of the sun (copper engraving by Bernard Picart, 1673–1733)
4 Portraits of the rulers of Peru from the first Inca King Manco Cápac (c. 1200; top left) and his sister-consort Mama Ocllo (top right) to King Ferdinand VI of Spain (1713–1759; bottom right).
5 The Puno Week celebrates the legendary emergence of Manco Cápac and Mama Ocllo from the waters of Lake Titicaca.

the people shouted with joy. "Viracocha sent his children Manco Cápac and Mama Ocllo, who was also Manco Cápac's consort, to the Isla del Sol in the middle of Lake Titicaca and gave them a golden rod as

According to legend, the god of creation, Viracocha, emerged from Lake Titicaca to create the sun. In Tiahuanaco he created not only the world but also Man.

"Once upon a time, long ago, the Earth lay in darkness. The people suffered indescribably from the absence of light and appealed in their prayers to their gods," wrote the Spanish chronicler Pedro Cieza de León. "Then the sun rose above Lake Titicaca in all its majesty and

legacy. They were to rise from the chilly waters of the lake, with the instructions, "Go wherever you like, and if you stop in order to eat and drink, push this rod into the earth. If it stays in the earth, settle at that place and rule the people with fairness, reason, patience, love and clemency." Manco Cápac and Mama Ocllo set off and reached the region of Cuzco, where the golden rod remained stuck in the ground and where they founded the Inca dynasties.

In fact, the Inca Empire began as a small principality in the Cuzco region around 1200. After the peoples expanded modestly in the immediate vicinity, around 1440 they set out, under the leadership of the Inca Pachacutec, to conquer more territories. Pachacutec reorganized the entire political structure of his dominion to create an efficiently organized centralized government.

Among the early conquests of the Inca was the region around

Lake Titicaca, where the Aymará lived for many centuries. The Inca declared the Isla del Sol a holy place only to be visited by members of the nobility. Here, at the place of their mythical origins, they worshiped the powerful sun deity Inti, who according to legend left a footprint on the island when ascending to heaven.

The name Inca originally referred only to the rulers, who were seen as the sons or earthly incarnation of the sun. As time passed the expression came to be used for victorious people as a whole who spoke Quechua.

The power of the Inca chieftains was absolute: the ruler was regarded as a divine being. Preservation of the divine lineage meant it was normal for brothers and sisters to marry. The Royal Council, which consisted of four Apu (prefects) followed the ruler, who as *Sapa Inca* stood at the head of the kingdom. The prefects ruled over the four divisions of the Kingdom of the Four World Regions (*Tahuantinsuyu*).

These "World Regions", corresponding to the four points of the compass, were divided into various provinces, which were ruled by *curaca*. They were in charge of the *puric*, who were in charge of a number of families which farmed the land in a sort of village community known as the *ayullu*.

The Isla del Sol is the mythical birthplace of the Inca, for it was here that Manco Cápac, the son of the god of creation, Viracocha, emerged from Lake Titicaca with his sister-consort Mama Ocllo to found the Inca people. From the landing stage Escalera del Inca ("Inca Staircase") in the southeast of the Isla del Sol, a staircase – quite steep in places – leads uphill to a spring, the Fuente del Inca y Milgrada. Here the water flows out of three openings in a rocky wall. Further south, the ruined Pilcocayna is a two-story square building, built with so-called "false" ceiling vaulting made of tiles stacked on top of each other. Through two trapezium-shaped gateways of the former Inca palace one obtains a magnificent view of the Cordillera Real and the twin peaks of holy Mount Illampú (6,368 m/20,756 ft and 6,427 m/ 21,081 ft).

Off the northwest tip of the island are the sunken ruins of Marka Pampa. The underwater ruins are 8 meters (26 feet)

beneath the surface of the lake in the middle of a triangle formed by the islands of Chullo, Pallalla and Koa. In Cha'llapampa on the Isla del Sol, amid the poverty-stricken huts and rusty shacks of corrugated iron, you can visit the magnificent treasures of Marka Pampa now housed in a whitewashed building that serves as a museum. Pottery from the Tiahuanaco period and stone chests dating from the Inca era, which were discovered during the 1970s, are on view.

On the little neighboring Isla de la Luna, most of the buildings open to visitors are in a very poor state of repair. The most important structure was the Acllahuasi, the Temple of the Sun Virgins. At its heart stood a female statue clothed in gold and silver; the walls of the temple were also clad in gold and silver leaf. All that is left of the temple – plundered on Pizarro's instructions – are ruins. The island was used as a prison until 1972.

The Inca Road Network

The most important links between the Inca capital Cuzco and the other parts of the empire comprised a network of roads running along the Andes in a north-south direction. Two main routes and countless branching tracks, created what is estimated to have made up a total of 20,000 kilometers (12,500 miles) of road. The first main route led across a distance of over 5,000 kilometers (3,125 miles) from South Colombia and Quito through the Andes to Cuzco and on to Chile; the second main route ran parallel to the first one along the coast. Both roads were linked to each other by numerous cross routes. Approximately every 30 kilometers (19 miles) was punctuated by tambos (rest houses) where messengers and relay runners (chasquis) could get food and drink as well as ojotas (running shoes) made of llama bladder. The Inca were able to transmit messages over a distance of up to 250 kilometers (156 miles) per day – an incredible achievement.

The Black Madonna of Copacabana

Within sight of the Isla del Sol and not far from the border with Peru, between the brown craggy hills of Cerro Calvario (Mount Calvary) and Cerro Sancollani that jut out into Lake Titicaca, is the most famous pilgrim destination of Andean Indian-Catholic culture: Copacabana, named Kota Kahuaña ("Lake View") when it was founded by the Inca Túpac Yupanqui during the 15th century on the site of a pre-Inca cult site.

Nowadays the little town is entirely dedicated to the Black Madonna. The image of Our Lady was created by Francisco Tito Yupanqui, a descendant of Túpac Yupanqui who received his training in a Catholic mission. He carved the Virgen de Copacabana

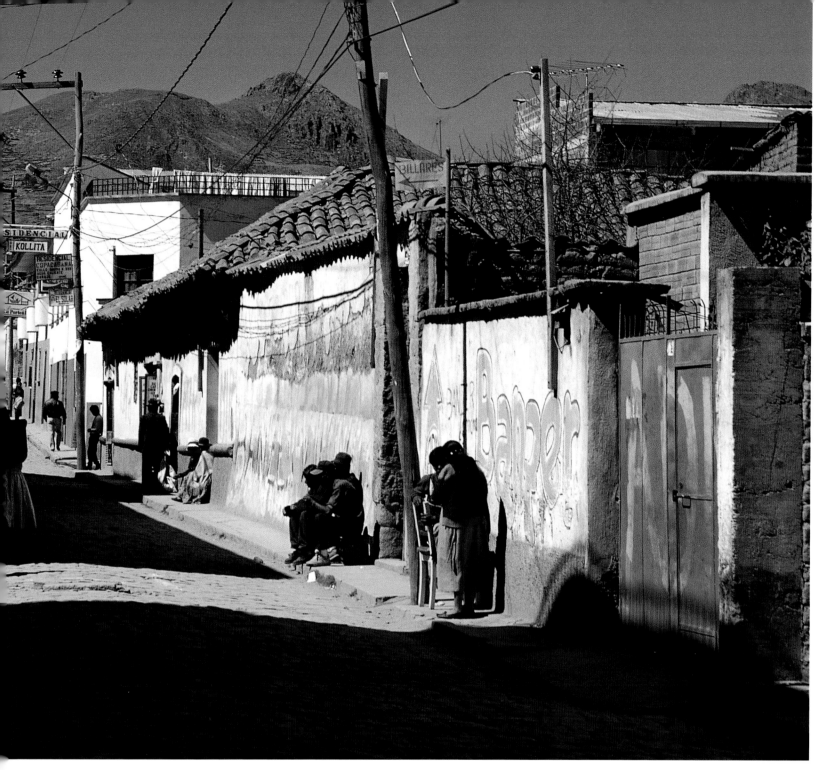

(also known as the Virgen Morena del Lago) out of agave wood. The statue of the Virgin Mary is about 1 meter (3.28 feet) in height with a complexion as dark as the faces of the market women on the square in front of the basilica. In a solemn procession in 1583 the figure was brought to Copacabana across Lake Titicaca on a raft. The Madonna figure with a crown of pure gold stands in a glass case on the first floor of the sacristy, behind the magnificent high altar. It can be admired from the nave during Mass. The Black Madonna was declared holy in 1925. Every year between 4th and 8th August, the faithful from the entire Andes region gather for the festival of the Coronation of the Virgin of Copacabana (Fiesta de la Virgen). Brazil's most famous beach in Rio de Janeiro was actually named after the little pilgrim town in honor of the Virgin.

The original little chapel erected in 1614 – 1618 for the Virgin of Copacabana was extended to become the elaborately decorated and magnificently decked out Basilica Copacabana. Construction is believed to have begun as early as 1670, but the cathedral was not completed until 1820. Its vast cross shape dominates the little town. The roofs and cupolas are tiled with Moorish mosaic stones in shades of terracotta. Countless traders have established themselves in front of the main entrance to the cathedral, selling paper decorations, flowers, beer, spirits and jewelry. Every Saturday and Sunday the square in front of the church is full of cars, buses and trucks elaborately decorated with flowers. A priest blesses the vehicles and the owners hope that they can depend on divine protection when driving.

65

Fact and Fiction

Historians and Writers in Peru

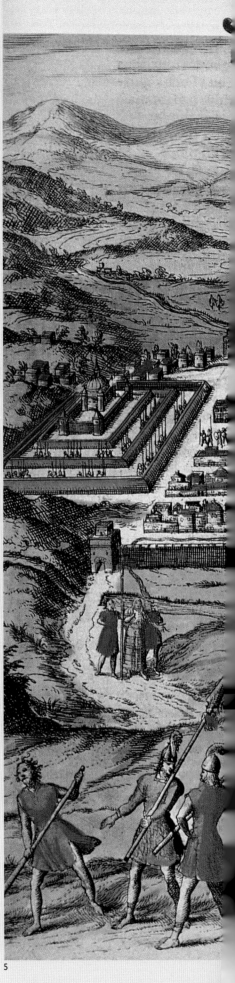

1 The self-portrait of Felipe Huamán Poma de Ayala (center) is one of around 400 drawings the chronicler used to illustrate his account of the life of the Inca and the Spanish conquest.
2 The famous chronicler Garcilaso de la Vega, whose mother was an Inca princess, was given the nickname "El Inca".
3 Portrait of the lyric poet César Vallejo. – 4 The writer Ricardo Palma was preserved for posterity on the Peruvian 10-Intis banknote.
5 Copper engraving of the Inca capital Cuzco from the atlas Civitates Orbis Terrarum of 1572.
6 Peru's most famous contemporary writer, Mario Vargas Llosa, during an election speech in 1990. He campaigned for the office of President, but lost the election.

The Inca had no written language, so much of what we know about them as a people can be traced back to the accounts of Spanish historians. One of the first important chroniclers of the New World was the mestizo Garcilaso de la Vega (1539–1616), son of a Spanish army general and an Inca princess. In 1560 he went to Spain, where at the end of his military career he wrote his main work, the *Comentarios Reales*, regarded as the prime source of Inca history. He based his information on what his mother related to him and a chronicle written by the priest Blas Valera, an Inca pupil of the Jesuits. De la Vega's *Royal Commentaries* were banned upon publication in 1609 in Seville.

Another important historian was the Spanish-born Pedro

CVSCO.

Cieza de León (1518–1560). He had close contact to members of the Inca and wrote several volumes on the history and culture of the Inca, as well as the conquest of Peru by the Spanish, under the title *Crónica del Perú (1550)* and *Segunda parte de la crónica del Perú (1553)*.

Huamán Poma Curi Occio (1534–1615), who became famous under the name Felipe Huamán Poma de Ayala, is

6

thought to have lived in Cuzco between 1554 and 1580. In his 1,200 pages long book, *El primer nueva crónica y buen gobierno*, he wrote between 1582 and 1613, he recorded the tales of his mother, who was a great-granddaughter of the Inca Túpac Yupanqui. Poma de Ayala's precious chronicle, which includes several hundred drawings, was long thought to have been lost but was discovered in a museum in Copenhagen in 1908.

More recent Peruvian literature is also concerned with the history of the country and its old myths and traditions, including the satirical tales *Tradiciones peruanas* by Ricardo Palma (1833-1919). The lyric poet César Vallejo (1892–1938) writes of the Indian legacy and experiences of the Spanish Civil War in his work.

Peru's most important contemporary writer is Mario Vargas Llosa, who was born in Arequipa in 1936. In 1990 he was a candidate for the presidency at the head of a liberal protest movement, but was defeated by his opponent Alberto Fujimori. Vargas Llosa works usually comprise a distinct political background, as was the case with one of his more recent works, *Lituma en los Andes* ("Death in the Andes"; 1993), which treats the bloody guerrilla war of the Sendero Luminoso and the recriminations of the militia and the army.

The Golden Navel of the World

Cuzco and the Inca Sites

Just as in western antiquity where, it was said, all roads once led to Rome, all Inca roads led to Cuzco – one of the most attractive towns in Peru and the epicenter of the lost Inca Empire. The Inca capital, which saw itself as the "Navel of the World" (*qosq'o*), lies more than 3,400 meters (11,152 feet) above sea level in a fertile valley in the eastern Andes. When the morning mist disperses and the sun climbs higher, the red-tiled roofs detach themselves more clearly from the surrounding mountains. In the thin mountain air the view is of the most brilliant clarity.

Apart from impressive pottery finds (above), Peru's treasures also include many ruins. The legendary Machu Picchu (center and large picture) is world famous. A flat temple stone symbolizes a condor, the sacred bird of the Inca (right).

From what the Spanish conquistadors and chroniclers wrote, we are told of the magnificence of the city walls in Inca times. Inca buildings are distinguished by a powerful, monumental matter-of-factness, their outer walls being completely devoid of exterior decoration. The interiors, by contrast, radiated magnificence and power with the walls bedecked in gold and silver. Similar to the glory of those interior walls palace and temple roofs were also burnished with gold.

Garcilaso de la Vega described the Inca capital and its inhabitants thus: "The ancient Inca kings divided Cuzco into quarters which resembled the four regions of their empire, which they called 'Tahuantinsuyu'. (...) And so the conquered peoples of the East had to live in the eastern districts of the town, and those from the West in the western section. Similarly, the peoples from the North and South had to live where they were ordered. (...) Going through the town you could thus see the entire empire and

the way it was made up of provinces, inhabitants and customs. And so it was with good reason that Cuzco was described as representing a model and the cosmography of the entire empire."

On the Plaza de Armas

The glittering former capital of an empire which once extended from Colombia to Argentina and Chile has retained a unique Indian atmosphere. The starting point of any walk through Cuzco is usually the Plaza de Armas in the center of town, where a fountain set in an attractive little park with trees and flower beds

The heritage of the Inca: The Intihuatana, the "Stone of the Sun," is the most important sacred relic of Machu Picchu (above); it was used to predict the solstices. Countless stairs and terraces lead to the Inca stronghold of Ollantaytambo (below). – The last Inca ruler Túpac Amaru was executed on the Plaza de Armas in Cuzco in 1572 (center).

recalls the decline of the Inca. The square looks idyllic enough today, but in 1572 it was the site of the execution of the last Inca ruler, Túpac Amaru I. Túpac Amaru II, whose real name was José Gabriel Condorcanqui and who led the last major Indian uprising, was also tortured to death on the Plaza de Armas in 1781.

Dominating the northeast side of the square is the mighty Cathedral whose twin towers rise to a height of 30 meters (98 feet). Situated at the location Viracocha's palace (the eighth Inca ruler) the cathedral took over a century to construct and the Spanish availed themselves of some of the massive andesite Inca blocks in the process. Standing in front of the cathedral, one cannot help but notice that the massive structure makes it look rather like a fortress. The two side doorways are decorated in rustic style, their gables framed by Spanish coats of arms. The largest bell in South America tolls in the left-hand tower. Only at night, when it is illuminated by spotlights to glow in a gentle

70

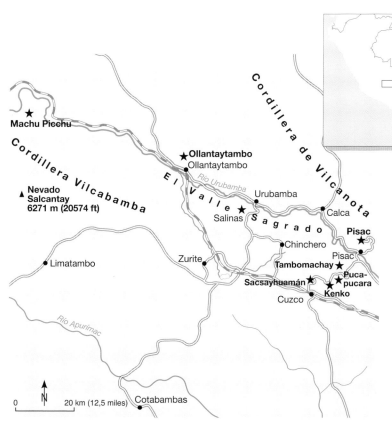

The market in the little Andean village of Pisac, which takes place every Sunday on the Plaza de Armas, is regarded as one of the most colorful in the land (left). Not far away, a herd of llamas crosses the plain of the Andes Highlands (below). Several times a day, a narrow-gauge railway chugs through the upper Urubamba Valley from Cuzco to the much-visited ruins of Machu Picchu (bottom).

yellow light, is the oppressive might of the building offset. One of the ten side chapels within contains a statue of the crucified Christ. From the time of the 1650 earthquake it has been revered as Señor de los Temblores (Lord of the Earthquakes). During Easter Week each year the Cuzqueños carry their patron saint through the streets in a solemn procession in the hope that he will protect them against earthquakes. The cathedral's imposing main altar was made of solid silver. It obscures the view of the original altar of carved cedar wood covered with gold which has been pushed to the back. The solid gold monstrance in the sacristy, inlaid with countless precious stones, was once another imposing sight but due to a theft it is no longer on view.

To the right of the Cathedral stands the El Triunfo church, named for the victory of the Spanish over the Inca led by Manco Cápac II in 1536. This was once the site of the Suntur Huasi round house, the most important Inca armory. Immediately behind the doorway stands the urn of the chronicler Garcilaso de la Vega (see page 66), although his earthly remains were taken back to Spain in 1978.

Diagonally opposite the cathedral is La Compañia, built between 1571 and 1668 by the Jesuits. A bitter quarrel arose between those who had commissioned the building and the other local priests concerning its completion, for many felt the edifice vied disrespectfully with the cathedral for importance. La Compañia occupies the site of Inca ruler Huayna Cápac's Amaru-Cancha palace and though narrower, it is similar in design to the

71

cathedral, yet the façade surpasses the latter in both elegance and harmony. The elaborately carved altar, ornamented with copious amounts of gold, is one of the loveliest in South America and bears witness – as do the other furnishings – to the vast wealth of those who built it.

Masterly Works of Art

Two other artistic treasures demonstrate the supremacy of this blend of Spanish colonial style and Indian craftsmanship. The first is the monastery church of La Merced, dating from the 16th century, boasting an ornately decorated and gilt high altar and Baroque cedar wood choir stalls. Another masterpiece is the monstrance, created in 1720, on exhibit in the monastery

72

museum. The shrine for the host is decorated with countless pearls, diamonds and other precious stones. In the passage between the church and the monastery hang two impressive paintings dating from colonial times. The work on the right depicts a battle between the Spanish conquistadors and the Araucan Indians in Chile, and the one on the left is a representation of the first South American martyr of the Order of the Blessed Virgin Mary of Mercy.

The second highpoint is the Church of San Blas, which is usually approached via the Calle Hatun Rumiyoc. The name stems from a twelve-sided stone in the city wall the street runs along – a remarkable example of the Inca's skill in constructing walls of huge stones without the use of mortar. The wall housing the Hatun Rumiyoc was once part of the Inca Roca palace. The mag-

nificent mansions of the Marquise Buenavista and Rocafuerte were built on top and subsequently inhabited by the Bishop of Cuzco. Nowadays it is the Museo de Arte Religioso exhibiting paintings, sculptures, furniture and folkloric objects.

If you continue up the street, at its end you will see the modest-looking Iglesia San Blas, founded in 1562 and built of adobe bricks. Inside is find one of the loveliest Baroque pulpits in the Andes, with elaborate cedar wood carving. The church itself was badly damaged by the earthquakes of 1650 and 1950, but the imaginatively carved Churrigueresque altars and monumental paintings of the Cuzco School (see page 76) have survived or been restored. The weight of the pulpit is borne by the figures of eight heretics who are on the verge of collapsing under their burden. Above it seven ghost-like figures resembling Greek masks

can be seen. The cornice base of the pulpit rests on 18 Baroque pillars supported by angels including the four apostles and the Virgin Mary.

A Temple of Gold

The church and monastery of Santo Domingo was built on top of the Coricancha, the largest sacred site of the Inca, the legendary Temple of the Sun. Unfortunately it was badly damaged during the 1950 earthquake. The last Inca ruler, Túpac Amaru I, is buried in a vault in the church.

Only three Spaniards saw the most famous temple in America, in its full glory. Sadly, they were the most ruthless members of Pizarro's band of robbers. They told of a massive gold altar weighing 190 pounds and a basin lined with 120 pounds of gold. Using their bare hands the conquistadors ripped 700 gold plates from the walls of the temple in order to accelerate the payment of the ransom for the Inca Atahualpa, whom they had taken prisoner. They left behind the most precious Inca symbol, a golden

image of the sun. It was mounted in such a way that it caught the rays of the morning sun and reflected them back into the glittering gold temple. Later, however, it disappeared.

Relics of a Lost World

Three kilometers (two miles) east of the center of Cuzco is the fortress complex of Sacsayhuamán, the only one of its kind in South America. Blocks of Cyclopean proportions, with hollowed-out and projecting angles, narrow passageways and remarkable plinths, form a triple fortifying wall.

Every year, on June 24, the Inti Raymi Festival (Sun Festival) is celebrated in the ruins of Sacsayhuamán. The celebration has been handed down from Inca times. On the day of winter solstice, the Inca and his court gathered with the entire population at dawn to greet the rising sun. The Inca and his Coya (sister, consort and Inca princess) were carried in a litter through the crowd, followed by the nobles and numerous Sun virgins bearing sacrificial gifts with hands stretched high above their heads. The

See page 81

Machu Picchu, the "Town in the Clouds" (large picture), was built during the 15th century. Since 1983 the ruins have been a UNESCO World Heritage site. Terraced fields at the entrance to the city indicate that the people here lived independently (left). There was even a prison in Machu Picchu (above).

Saints in Inca Costume

The Cuzco School

1 and 3 Magnificent wall paintings by the Cuzco pupil Luis de Riano adorn the interior of the Jesuit church in Andahuaylillas. 2 In the church in Curahuara in the Altiplano of Bolivia, a fresco of the Archangel Michael dating from the 17th century decorates the interior. – 4 In the painting in the mission church of St Francis Xavier in Bolivia, Indians and Jesuit priests at the mission station and the priest who built the church, Pater Martin Schmid, are grouped around St Paul. 5 This picture of the Virgin Mary by an unknown artist can be seen in the Casa Real de la Moneda in Potosí, Bolivia. – 6 The portrait of an Inca nobleman from the colonial era is exhibited in the Inca Museum of Cuzco.

There was a huge demand for pictures to decorate the numerous churches, monasteries and palaces built in the vice regal region of Peru during the second half of the 16th century. Bernardo Bitti, born in 1548 in Italy and a pupil of Raphael, was sent to Peru in 1573 with instructions to "paint beautiful pictures in order to impress the natives who are receptive for the majesty of the characters portrayed." When Bitti realized just how many religious paintings would be needed, he

began to instruct Indígenas and Mestizos in Cuzco in European painting techniques.
As their experience and self-confidence increased, the native artists distanced themselves commensurately from their models and rather than

76

5

6

European traits the saints they painted resembled mestizos. Their robes were adorned with precious necklaces and gold as in Inca times, and the archangels carried Spanish weapons.

Thus a completely new art form developed in Cuzco during the 17th century, combining European elements with the viewpoint of the Indígenas. It became famous as the Estilo Escuela Cusqueña (Cuzco School). The artists especially liked to paint pictures of the Virgin Mary – with or without the Infant Jesus – and the Holy Family, as well as saints and archangels.

The sacristy of Cuzco Cathedral features a huge painting by mestizo artist Marcos Zapata. Depicting the Last Supper, with Christ and the Twelve Apostles dining on roast guinea pig and chicha corn beer and a dark-skinned Judas it displays the unmistakable influence of the Indian view of the universe.

Pérez de Holguín (1660–1724) from Potosí in Bolivia was also influenced by Zapata, who founded the Potosí School of Painting and whose style is above all characterized by light and dark effects. He created the painting Virgen del Cerro in the Casa Real de Moneda in Potosí. The museum of the Santa Teresa convent exhibits pictures from his early phase that feature concealed self-portraits of the artist.

One of the most important representatives of the Escuela Cusqueña is Diego Quispe Tito (1611 – 1681), whose paintings can be seen in Cuzco Cathedral, the Museo de Arte Religioso and in the monastery church of Santo Domingo. Tito's are the first works of landscape representations in the history of Peruvian art. Mestizo's were forbidden to sign their works so he marked them with pictures of hats without an owner and jungle birds.

77

Farmhouse surrounded by fields in the Andean Highlands.

Huge stone blocks were transported to Sacsayhuamán to build the Inca fortress (large photo). This is the setting for the grandiose annual Inti Raymi Festival (right).– In Quenco a sacred Inca site is hidden away inside a rock (above).

80

highlight of the ceremony was the sacrifice of a llama. Today Inti Raymi is presented as a vast historical pageant.

A few kilometers east of Sacsayhuamán you can see the most impressive examples of typical Inca stonework in Quenco. A rock of weathered limestone is covered with zig-zag grooves, which enhance the natural shape of the rock. A narrow pass curving above the smooth rock walls leads to a cave in which altars and seats have been hewn in the solid rock. A tall rock in the middle was obviously the center of a religious cult. Via a steep path you can return to the main road with a magnificent view of the snow-capped peak of Auzangate (6,336 meters/ 20,782 feet) to the southeast.

From Quenco the route continues to Pucapucara, a little Inca fortress and former post station, in which travellers could find a bed and store their goods temporarily.

Just a few hundred meters further on lie the ruins of Tambo-machay, also known as the Baths of the Inca. Ritual cleansings may have been carried out here. It is also thought that tired Inca messengers rested here and refreshed themselves in the turquoise blue waters which flow out from an underground spring behind one of the four terrace-like walls to fill a series of pools.

In the Sacred Valley of the Inca

The valley of the Río Urubamba between Pisac and Ollantaytambo, the Valle Sagrado de los Incas (Sacred Valley of the Inca), is one of the scenic and cultural highlights of Peru.

A steep rocky spur juts out from the snow-capped Andes into the Urubamba Valley. Here, between the Río Vilcanota and the little Chongo River, some 300 meters (984 feet) above Pisac, rises one of the largest Inca mountain fortress surrounded by steep rock walls. The temple complex, extending over many square kilometers, is one of the best-preserved Inca ruins to be found anywhere. The center of the complex is the sacred area containing remains of palaces, temples and burial places. Here, too, is the

81

In the Sacred Valley of the Inca: In the salinas the local citizens hack away at the salt in hundreds of basins which the Incas used before them (right). – Above the Río Urubamba rise the ruins of Pisac (below). – The women of Urubamba wear tall white hats (right-hand page, below).

Cruel Oracles

Every day, in the early morning hours, a llama was sacrificed in Cuzco to the sun god Inti. The victim had to be looking eastwards when it was killed. First of all the priest stabbed it in the throat; then he opened the breast and ripped out lungs, kidneys and liver. By studying the inner organs the priest then interpreted the oracle while the blood was sprinkled over the statues of the deities.

At solemn festivals a human sacrifice was usual in Cuzco. Prisoners of war or the children of vanquished tribes would be chosen for this purpose. But boys and girls from aristocratic Inca families would also be selected and led in a festive procession to the sacrificial altar. The children were anaesthetized with coca and then suffocated; finally their hearts were removed.

sun shrine Intihuatana, a rock carved by a masterly sculptor into the form of a cone and which, like a sundial, served to determine the seasons and the times for sowing seeds and bringing in the harvest. A bath, erected for ritual purposes, at the southern end of the temple city, was fitted out with steps for climbing in as well as hand-holds carved into the rock face.

Machu Picchu – the Lost City

According to legend, the Spanish did not actually receive all the gold which Atahualpa had promised them in 1532 for his release from captivity (see page 99). When they heard that Atahualpa had been murdered, the Incas reputedly hid most of it in the mountains – perhaps in the legendary refuge of Vilcabamba in the

Andes to the west of Cuzco, the place from where the Inca prince Manco Cápac II led a desperate resistance against the Spanish conquistadors until he, too, was killed in 1544. The American historian Hiram Bingham set out to find the lost city of Vilcabamba some 90 years ago.

As leader of an expedition, he set out from Cuzco in 1911 and climbed into the narrow Urubamba Gorge, where the Indian who guided him for days along a narrow mule path told him the story of an abandoned city perched above steep rocky walls. After a difficult climb past abandoned ruins and fertile terraced fields, Bingham suddenly found himself in a maze of white granite walls. He had discovered an Inca city which was largely overgrown with jungle but virtually intact. Even the Spanish had failed to find it: Machu Picchu.

At the colorful market of Chinchero (large photo), vegetables and potatoes grown in the fields of the Urubamba Valley are the main goods for sale (right-hand page, below). Lambs also change hands (right). – In the central highland artichokes grow up to an altitude of 3,400 meters (1,115 feet; right-hand page, top).

The "City in the Clouds", as it was known, stands on a U-shaped promontory with steep slopes perched at an altitude of 2,400 meters (7,872 feet) surrounded by tropical vegetation. On three sides it is protected by the Río Urubamba and on the fourth by the cone of the 2,743 meter high (8,997 feet) Huayna Picchu. Whether Machu Picchu, today one of the greatest sights of South America, was a refuge, a sacred place or the country estate of an Inca, are just some of the questions which will remain for ever unanswered.

84

Market day in Pisac and Chinchero

After all that history and culture the colorful Sunday market in Pisac provides an opportunity to learn something about the everyday lives of the Indígenas. Goods of every description are offered for sale: animals and fabrics, fruit and vegetables, pots and tools, medicinal herbs and llama embryos which are offered when a house is built, and a wide range of handicrafts. Weaving, pottery and carving attract customers from the nearby towns as well as tourists.

The headgear worn by the market women is particularly attractive. The shapes and colors betray the origins of the wearer: Cuzqueñas wear a sort of doctor's hat while the hats from Pisac are gently curved. The women with the stiff white hats decorated with colored bands also come from the area. You can recognize the women from nearby Chinchero by the borders around the top of their hats. The flat felt hats of the Quechua women from the highlands around Cuzco are decorated with sparkling braid trimming.

Another colorful market is also held on Sundays in Chinchero. The town lies on higher ground above the Urubamba Valley, affording a magnificent view of the hilly Altiplano and the snow-capped peaks of the Vilcabamba and Urubamba cordilleras on the horizon.

The Andean Highlands near Chinchero.

1

With Drums and Flutes

The Music of the Andes

2

1 and 2 Among the oldest musical instruments in the Andes are the many different varieties of flute.
3 String instruments like the charango were introduced by the Spanish conquistadors.
4 In the towns and villages of the central Andes Highlands, colorful folklore festivals with lively music and dancing are held all the year round.
5 At the impressive Inti Raymi Festival in Cuzco and Sacsayhuamá, magnificently costumed bands perform with drums and zampoñas.
6 A dance performance at a folklore festival in Chinchero
7 The charango, a sort of miniguitar, and the zampoña, a pan flute, generate a festive atmosphere in no time.

Whenever the conversation turns to Peruvian folk music, everyone always thinks of the song "El Condor Pasa". However, few people are aware that the song, made popular in 1970 by Paul Simon and Art Garfunkel with the Los Incas group, was actually written by the Peruvian composer Daniel Alomia Robles, for an operetta in 1913.

As pictures of musicians on old drinking vessels show, music was played in the Andes Highlands long before the Spanish conquest. The music of the Andes, with its typical melancholy pentatonic melodies, often sounds foreign and exotic to European ears; however, it is

for this very reason that the nostalgic sounds of the Peruvian pan flute are so popular among tourists.

The *zampoña* is a pan flute made of a single or double row of whistles of varying length and diameter which are closed at the bottom end. The lips of the player brush across the pipes and thus produce the

characteristic, plaintive sounds of the pentatonic scale. Among the various wind instruments played in the Andes is the *quena*, a vertical flute made of reed or wood and with a carved mouthpiece; it often has six holes on the top and one at the back for the thumb. Other verti-

cal flutes include the *pinkillo*, which is made of reed and produces a high, almost shrill tone, and the *tarka*, made of wood. It is frequently heard during the Carnival season and can produce two notes simultaneously. String instruments were first brought to Peru by the Spanish

3

drumsticks. Cylinder drums of varying sizes exist, either with one skin (*huancara*) or with two (*tinya*), on the underside of which there is sometimes a string for scraping.

6

5

7

and then further developed by the Indígenas. Amongst which is the *charango*, a string instrument resembling a small guitar. The sound box was originally made from the shell of an armadillo; today it is made of wood. The player plucks at the six pairs of gut or metal strings and produces a high sound. The Andean harp (*arpa llanera*) has 36 strings and covers five octaves of the diatonic sale. Indígena music also uses the *bombo*, a deep bass drum covered with goat or llama skin. Like the kettle drum in a village band, it is played using padded

89

In Search of Vanished Cultures

The Coast of Peru

Timeless beauties: a golden item of jewelry decorated with turquoise from the Museo d'Oro in Lima (above) and an ornate tile mosaic from the colonial era (below).

When Francisco Pizarro founded Lima in January 1535, he and his 13 commanders retained the right to build houses around the central square in the new city. So there arose on the Plaza Mayor, in the Old City of Lima, an ensemble of colonial monuments. Pizarro's palace is no longer standing; since 1938, the site has been occupied by the monumental neo-classical Palacio de Gobierno, which is the official residence of the President of the Republic.

Also on Plaza Mayor stands the mighty cathedral, whose foundation stone was laid by Pizarro. It had to be completely rebuilt following the devastating earthquake of 1746. The neighboring Palacio de Arzobispo and its exquisitely carved balconies was built in 1924. Opposite are the city administrative offices, built in 1945 also featuring wooden balconies.

Today the major companies, exclusive shops, gourmet restaurants, and luxury hotels are to be found in the new suburbs of San Isidro and Miraflores. The wide avenues, glass and concrete high-rises, and green spaces with fountains of Miraflores in

The "Three Graces" in the capital, Lima, radiate contemporary charm (above). – Far from the bustle of the big city, the fishermen in Huanchaco mend their nets in the manner of their ancestors, by hand, before heading out to sea again in their reed boats, affectionately known as caballitos – "ponies" (right-hand page).

particular, radiate a contemporary, cosmopolitan air. The Costa Verde, a district of Miraflores popular with surfers, attracts customers to elegant restaurants like the "Rosa Nautica", built on stilts above the Pacific surf.

In the "City of Springtime"

From Lima, the Panamericana heads northwards past the popular resort of Ancón and through a rather monotonous desert landscape to Huaura, where the freedom fighter José de San Martín proclaimed Peru's independence on July 28, 1821.

The ruined city of Paramonga stands on a hill a few kilometers beyond Pativilca. The view from here extends for miles across the valley planted with sugar cane. A sprawling burial site nearby recalls the last battle of the Chimú against the attacking troops of the Inca Túpac Yupanqui.

The center of Trujillo, the second-largest city in Peru with a population of more than half a million, has retained the magnificent architecture of the Spanish colonial era. Spacious squares, elaborately decorated churches and elegant houses in Hispano-Moorish style characterize the Ciudad de la Primavera (City of Springtime), as Trujillo is known for its pleasant climate. No sightseer should fail to include the many historic patrician

houses on his list of priorities. The colonial villas, painted in pastel colors, are often adorned with elaborate wrought-iron window gratings.

In 1820 the city was the first in Peru to declare its independence from the Spanish. It was here that Simón Bolívar prepared his campaigns which four years later led to the end of Spanish rule in the Battle of Ayacucho.

In the early mornings in the little fishing village of Huanchaco, the fishermen sit astride their reed boats and hold a long bamboo pole as they head out to sea. They call their boats *caballitos de totora* – "reed ponies."

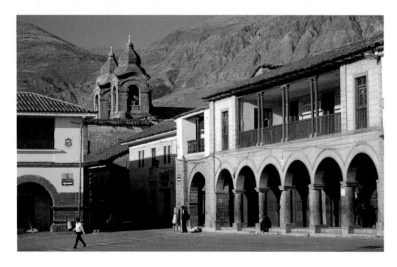

Taking a break in Chivay (above). The Costa Verde off Lima is popular with surfers (center). Ayacucho is regarded as one of the loveliest colonial towns in Peru (below).

Clay Temples and Princely Graves

From Trujillo it is not far to Chan Chan, the capital of the former Chimú Empire, which once encompassed the entire coast, from Tumbes on the present-day border with Ecuador as far as the Val-

BRAZIL

Chiclayo
★ Sipán
Cajamarca

La Huaca
Arco Iris ★
Huanchaco ★
Río Moche
Chan-Chan ★ ★ La Huaca del Sol
Trujillo ★
Moche ★ La Huaca de la Luna

Pucallpa

Cordillera

Río Marañón
Alpamayo 5947 m
(19511 ft)

Chimbote
Río Santa
Huascarán
6768 m (22205 ft)

Casma
Huaraz

Huánuco

Goyllarisquizga

Paramonga ★
Pativilca

Huaura

Río Apurímac
Río Urubamba
Río Yavero

La Oroya
PERU
Río Chillón
Ancón

Lima
Pachacamac ★

Quillabamba

Huancavelica
Machu Picchu ★

Ayacucho

Cuzco

Islas Ballestas

Nevado
Auzangate
6336 m (20787 ft)

Pisco
Península
de Paracas
Ica

Andes

Nazca Lines ★ Nazca

Cruz del Cóndor ★
Cañón del Colca ★

Río Colca
Nevado
Chachani
6075 m
(19931 ft)
Nevado Misti
5835 m
(19144 ft)
Arequipa

Pacific Ocean

ley of the Río Chillon to the north of Lima. The golden age of Chan Chan was in the 13th and 14th centuries, when it became the first major city in South America. Up to 100,000 citizens are estimated to have lived in the adobe houses, which were built of air-dried clay bricks.

The royal city was built along symmetrical lines. Its temples were adorned with reliefs of large-scale ornaments or mythological figures carved from damp clay. The city was divided into several palace districts surrounded by high walls and each reserved for the members of a particular profession. It is worth visiting the restored palace complex named after the Swiss explorer of South America Johann Jakob von Tschudi.

A large fleet of fishing boats lies anchored at Paita on the northern coast. The harbor is one of the biggest fishing ports in the country (above). – A lunch date? A number of attractive restaurants in Ayacucho can fit the bill (below).

93

On the way to Chan Chan visitors should make a point of exploring the Huaca La Esmeralda near Masiche. The "Emerald Temple" of the Chimú is decorated with exotic patterns and animal symbols. Furthermore the richly decorated walls of the Templo del Arco Iris (Rainbow Temple), alternatively dubbed the Huaca del Dragón (Dragon Temple), for the subject matter of its reliefs being dominated by numerous rainbows and dragons should not be avoided. The sacred sites of Huaca del Sol and Huaca de la Luna (Pyramid of the Sun and Pyramid of the Moon) south of Trujillo date from the Moche (*Mochica*) era, which extended from about the beginning of the Christian era until approx. 600 AD. This region was at the center of its civilization. At its height, the Moche culture extended even further to the north than Chiclayo. In 1987, the largest hoard of gold ever discovered in America was found at Sipán, east of Chiclayo. The 1,500-year-old grave of a prince known as the Señor de Sipán contained a headdress, a breastplate, chain, death mask and earrings – all of solid gold. Archaeologists discovered more graves nearby including that of the "Old Lord of Sipán" and a priest.

The Ruins of Pachacamac

The Pan Americana highway continues south from Lima directly through a brownish-yellow lunar landscape, skirting tall sand dunes and passing through tiny hamlets studded with brightly colored houses. Little roadside stands sell bananas and oranges, nuts and drinks along the way.

From the 9th century Pachacamac was an important pilgrimage site for the peoples of the coast and the highlands and was most likely the chief city of a powerful kingdom around 1000 AD. The most valuable find in the ruined city is an exquisitely carved wooden column representing Pachacamac, the god of creation of the coastal people. It is thought that sun virgins lived in the Casa de las Mamaconas, which dates from the Inca period. The remains of the pre-Incan Pachacamac Temple stand on a smaller hill and its clay walls still bear traces of painted decorations. The Sun Temple of the Inca stands on a second, taller hill. From here you have a spectacular view across the ruined city to the Pacific Ocean.

The cityscape of Trujillo is determined by attractive colonial-style houses with decorative window bars (above); the pretty inner courtyards abound in luxuriant greenery (left). Taking a short rest in Caraz (below).

See page 100

Rocky coast on the Paracas peninsula.

The Death of the Inca King

The End of Atahualpa in Cajamarca

1 This balcony clings to the house in Cajamarca like a swallow's nest. – 2 There is always time for a chat in the town in the Andean Highlands. The people here wear white straw hats for protection against the scorching sun.
3 Atahualpa, the last Inca ruler before the country was conquered by Pizarro (colored etching dated 1673).
4 The capture of Atahualpa on November 16, 1532 (colored lithograph after a drawing by August C. Haun, 1855–1894).
5 The Cuarto del Rescate, in which Atahualpa was kept prisoner, is a mute witness from past Inca times. – 6 Idyll with fountain and cactus: a pretty courtyard in Cajamarca.

Rumours of fabulous hoards of gold compelled Francisco Pizarro to leave Panama in 1531 and conquer the vast Inca Empire with a tiny army of barely more than 180 mercenaries, 60 horses and a handful of guns. The Spaniard and his men reached Cajamarca in the northern Andean Highlands on November 15, 1532. Still some distance away they could see the Inca ruler's enormous camp at Atahualpa, which the king had established on the way from Quito to Cuzco. He had only recently conquered his half-brother Huáscar and imprisoned him in Cuzco after a bitter war of succession which had lasted for five years.

Pizarro sent his brother Hernando and the conquistador Hernando de Soto to Atahualpa. When the two Spanish commanders returned they

98

5

6

related with dismay that the Inca (unlike the Aztecs in Mexico) showed no superstitious fears of the strange white men. In spite of the overwhelming numerical superiority of the Incas, an army of 50,000 soldiers had been gathered,

Pizarro ordered his people to capture Atahualpa on his return the next day.

Pedro Pizarro, a cousin of the conquistador, described the events of November 16, 1532: "When Marquis Don Francisco Pizarro saw that Atahualpa too was approaching the Plaza, he sent the priest Fray Vicente de Valverde ... to meet Atahualpa, in order to bid him in the name of God and the King to submit himself to the law of Our Lord Jesus Christ and His Majesty's service. The padre used a missal, from which he read, and when Atahualpa saw him, he asked if he could look at it. The Padre closed the book and gave it to Atahualpa; holding it in his hand, but not knowing how to open it, he threw it to the ground."

This was the signal for the Spanish to rush out of their ambush and to attack the Indians, who were completely caught off their guard. Atahu-alpa was held prisoner in the "Cuarto del Rescate," the "Ransom Room". To secure his release he offered to fill the room, which measured 60 square meters (646 square feet) up to the height of his out-stretched hands with gold, silver and jewelry. The Inca kept his word, and to this day you can see the dark line on the wall which marked the height of the treasure. The Spanish conquistadors took possession of the treasure greedily – and still sentenced the Inca to death, purportedly for treason. Atahualpa was executed by the Spanish on the Plaza de Armas in Cajamarca on 29 August 1533.

99

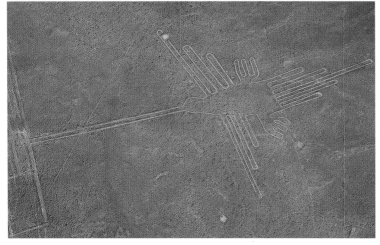

In the middle of the desert: the Hua-cachina Oasis (above). – Mystery pictures: humming bird near Nazca (below) and "El Candelabro" on Paracas (right).

Islands in the "Stormy Wind"

Visitors to Pisco may well find themselves thinking of the national drink of Peru, Pisco Sour, a cocktail made of local brandy (pisco), lime juice and a little sugar. But the town is even more famous as the starting point for excursions to the Paracas Peninsula, the Quechua name meaning "Stormy Wind."

On Paracas in 1927 archaeologists discovered a series of tombs containing 429 mummies wrapped in elaborately woven shrouds. Some of the skulls had been chiseled open and sealed afterward with a gold plate; evidence of trepanation – an operation on the head carried out while the subject was still alive. The remains are those of the 3,000-year-old Paracas Culture.

Off the Paracas Peninsula are the islands of the Ballestas archipelago. Taking a boat trip there enables the visitor to see not only sea lions and seals on the Islas Ballestas, but also Humboldt

penguins, pelicans, cormorants, boobies, sea swallows and sea-gulls. As one approaches the Paracas peninsula by boat a huge geoglyph shaped like a three-armed candelabra comes into view, on a slope on the southern tip of the peninsula. To this day, scientists are still trying to work out the meaning of El Candelabro.

A Miracle in the Desert

Ica, the center of the wine-growing region, is actually located in the middle of the desert. Surrounded by vast sand dunes, the town sprawls out across the valley of the Río Ica. This is where the famous Pisco grapes and other fine vintages ripen. A few kilometers from Ica, beside a small lake the oasis of Huacachina appears like a mirage in the midst of sand dunes. It is purported that the greenish waters, rich in sulfur and minerals contain healing properties for rheumatism and skin complaints.

101

Seals, sealions (right), and penguins (bottom) frolic on the Islas Ballestas. Thanks to the Humboldt current Pelicans also find plenty to eat off the coast of Peru (below). They are skilful sailors and prefer, above all, to dine on sardines.

The Pottery of the Moche Culture

In the Trujillo region, the pottery placed beside the dead as grave goods renders a revealing picture of the lifestyle of the warlike Moche (Mochica) who once inhabited this area. Many of the skillfully worked clay sculptures portray people engaged in everyday activities. Especially famous are the elegant portrait vases which feature realistic representations of individuals. War was a particularly popular theme for the Moche and was depicted in battle scenes stocked with crowds of figures demonstrating great attention to detail. Other vessels use mythical or erotic motifs and animals and plants. Moche ceramics were produced in an imaginative variety of forms, most with a stirrup spout. The main colour was brick red on an ivory background after which brown and black shades were added.

The Colca Canyon is one of the deepest in the world and home to the Andean condor (above). Fishermen in the port of Callao, which belongs to Lima (below).

In 1939, U.S. scientist Paul Kosok spotted some strange lines as he flew over the desert plateau near Nazca. They have been dubbed geoglyphs and are huge representations of animals and geometric patterns. The lines are gouged to a depth of 20 centimeters (8 inches) and 1 meter (3,28 feet) wide out of the dark earth and their actual form is only recognizable from the air. The German researcher Maria Reiche, who studied the mysterious 2,000-year-old lines for over 50 years up to her death in 1998, was convinced that they represented an astronomical calendar. The animal signs possibly representat constellations. In 1994 UNESCO included the geoglyphs in the list of World Heritage Sites.

The Valley of the Condor

Arequipa lies inland, on the edge of a 200 kilometer long (125-mile) chain of volcanoes. Its houses and churches of white trass, have attractively ornate façades. Immediately behind the town, the twin volcanoes Misti (5,835 m/ 19,139 ft) and Chachani (6,075 m/ 19,926 ft) rise majestically to the heavens.

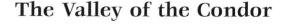

No visit to Peru's "White City" can be complete without including a trip to the Cañón del Colca, the "Valley of the Condors", around 150 kilometers (94 miles) north of Arequipa. The deep erosion of the volcanic massifs caused by the Río Colca has created a spectacular canyon with remarkable scenery. The entire cañón is covered with terraces. Nowhere else can offer a better view of the majestic flight of the Andean condor than the observation terrace Cruz del Cóndor, 1,200 meters (3,936 feet) above the Río Colca.

*Pillars, gables and friezes adorn
the 300-year-old white trass façade
of the Jesuit church La Compañia
on the Plaza de Armas in Arequipa (right).
On the outskirts of town or on the
market: almost always visible on
the horizon of the city are the
snow-capped summits of the volcanoes Chachani (above) and Misti
(below).*

Beach cottages in Colán on the northern coast.

The Town of the Nuns

The Santa Catalina Convent in Arequipa

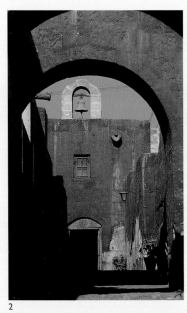

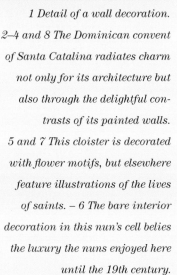

1 Detail of a wall decoration. 2–4 and 8 The Dominican convent of Santa Catalina radiates charm not only for its architecture but also through the delightful contrasts of its painted walls. 5 and 7 This cloister is decorated with flower motifs, but elsewhere feature illustrations of the lives of saints. – 6 The bare interior decoration in this nun's cell belies the luxury the nuns enjoyed here until the 19th century.

The Convento Santa Catalina, over 400 years old, was founded in 1580. In the 17th century the complex expanded to an area of more than 20,000 square meters (215,200 square feet). Surrounded by high walls, the convent's buildings, yards and alleys form a proper "town within a town".

The convent, for which Maria de Guzmán, a wealthy widow, had purchased the land, belonged to the Dominican order and had the strictest entrance qualifications of all the monasteries and convents in Peru. To gain admittance to the convent the novices had to be from upper-class Spanish families and bring a large dowry. The money was needed, among other things, to secure the board and lodgings of the large number of servants who made it possible for these daughters of wealthy origins to maintain a pleasant lifestyle within the convent, in which of course the vow of poverty at least officially applied. At least 400 of the 500 or more women, who lived here during the 17th and 18th centuries, were servants.

108

8

6

7

It is not generally known what actually happened behind the high walls of Santa Catalina. But Pope Pius IX finally put an end to the luxurious living. In 1871 he sent the Dominican nun Maria Josefa Cadena to Arequipa with the task of restoring monastic order in Santa Catalina. She returned all the dowries to the families of the nuns and fired all the servants. Convento Santa Catalina has been open to the public only since 1970. The Hispanic-Moorish architecture gives the visitor the feeling that time has stood still here. The walls of the convent buildings are offering a charming contrast of white trass and vibrant brown, blue and ochre tones. Today, around 20 nuns live in one section of the convent. Tourist entrance fees are used to pay for the maintenance of the convent complex.

109

Charming Towns and Natural Beauty

The Bolivian Altiplano

The antara is a pan flute made of a single row of whistles.

Bolivia's capital, La Paz, is located in a basin near the eastern edge of the Altiplano 3,700 meters (12,136 feet) above sea level. Tucked away in the Andes, its population of over one million makes it not only the largest city in the country, but also the highest metropolis in the world. As the country's economic and administrative center it has long since overtaken Sucre as the capital of the country, although the latter officially continues to bear the title to this day.

La Paz was originally founded as *La Ciudad de Nuestra Señora de la Paz* (The City of Our Lady of Peace) in October 1548 in Laja, 30 kilometers (19 miles) from its present site. Only three days later, however, the newly founded city was moved to its present location, the site where the Aymará had previously inhabited who discovered gold in the Río Choqueyapu.

Ceja de El Alto – The Eyebrow of El Alto – as the higher part of the El Alto suburb is called, features brightly painted houses and shacks clinging to its slopes where poorer sections of the population, often without electricity supplies, are accommodated. From their miserable balcony they can stare down on the spick-and-span districts below, where the wealthy Bolivians, the diplomats, and significant members of the military withdraw to in luxury. At the center in between, around the Plaza Murillo, is the historic heart of the city with its array of colonial mansions, churches, government buildings and modern high-rises.

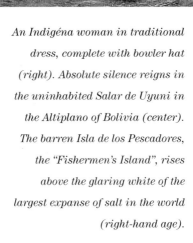

An Indigéna woman in traditional dress, complete with bowler hat (right). Absolute silence reigns in the uninhabited Salar de Uyuni in the Altiplano of Bolivia (center). The barren Isla de los Pescadores, the "Fishermen's Island", rises above the glaring white of the largest expanse of salt in the world (right-hand age).

110

Potosí and the Treasure of the "Silver Mountain"

During the 17th century Potosí, perched on the inhospitable high plateau of the Andes, was the wealthiest and largest city in South America. The silver mines transformed the settlement, and it was elevated to the rank of Villa Imperial, a glittering city with gold decorated churches, city palaces with luxurious interiors and streets paved with silver cobblestones.

The town on the magic silver mountain Sumaj Orcko, soaring almost 800 meters (2,624 feet) above Potosí dubbed by the Spanish Cerro Rico (Rich Mountain) for its inexhaustible deposits of silver, wallowed in indescribable luxury. At the end of the 18th century, however, the wealth was exhausted – although the search for ore in Cerro Rico continues to this day. At Potosí's center is the Plaza 10 de Noviembre, dominated by the monumental cathedral, built between 1806 and 1836 on the site of the original building, which had collapsed. The neo-classical building has three naves supported by massive alabaster pillars and side chapels on a scale which is virtually unmatched in the whole of Bolivia.

But Potosí's most famous building is the Casa Real de la Moneda, completed in 1773 after the old building, dating from 1572,

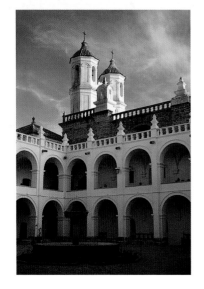

The Indígena women wear their finest dresses for the fiesta Nuestro Señor Jesús del Gran Poder in La Paz (above). – Nature also presents its most attractive side at the Laguna Colorada, enchanting travelers with its constantly changing interplay of colors (center). – The Convento San Felipe Neri in Sucre, its church crowned by twin towers, is a jewel of neo-colonial architecture (right).

had become too small. It is the largest secular building in the former vice-regal region of Peru. The fortress-like building of the Mint, where the Viceroy's coins were fabricated, served alternately as a fortress and a prison following Bolivia's independence. Today the Casa Real de la Moneda is a museum, where aside from the old minting machines colonial era furniture, religious art and archaeological finds from Tiahuanaco, are on display (see page 54–57). The massive main façade of the building is broken up by the Mannerist portal and its pillars, windows, balcony bearing a Spanish coat of arms. The entire Mint complex is grouped around three pretty patios surrounded by arcades. In the first courtyard a huge mask of Bacchus, the god of food and wine, smiles down at the observer seeming to symbolize the city and its lost wealth.

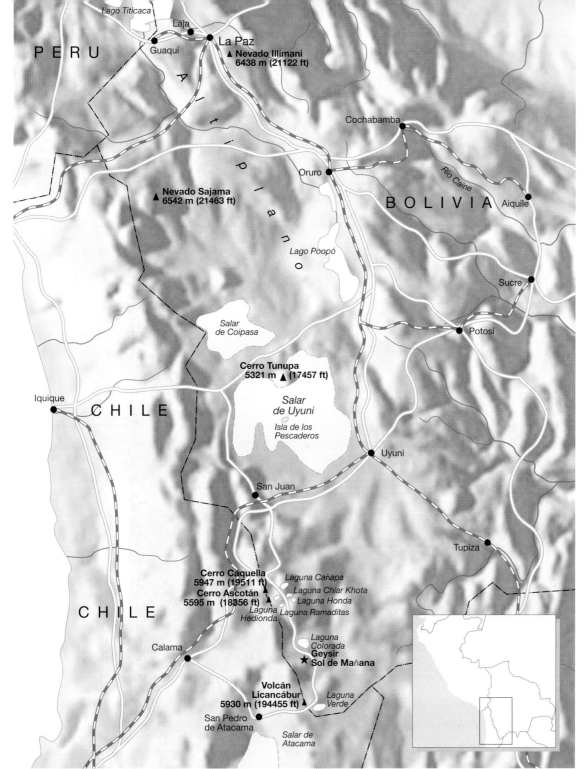

The colors and shapes of the hats and caps worn by the Indígenas in the Andean Highlands seem inexhaustible.

The most prominent colonial church in Potosí, the Iglesia San Lorenzo de los Carangas, dominates the Mercado Central. It is a masterpiece of Mestizo Baroque dating from 1548. The doorway is a particular high point, luxuriantly adorned with tropical plant motifs. Turned column figures are worked into the main pillar, displaying sun, moon and stars and two masks in the form of Indian deities. The interior of the church has a fine silver altar and paintings by Melchor Pérez de Holguín, the founder of the Potosí School of Painting (see page 77).

Thick monastery walls surround the Convento y Museo Santa Teresa on the Plaza Vicuñas, which was completed in 1691. It is run by Carmelite nuns. The convent museum shows a dimly lit refec-tory in which a skull serves to remind the nuns of the transitory nature of all earthly existence. On the upper floor, in the castigo, the punishment room, a collection of iron chains and a cross covered with nails are on view. The picture gallery shows a number of paintings from Holguín's early phase, which contain hidden self-portraits of the artist. From Santa Teresa it is not far to the Arco de Cobija, a triumphal arch which once separated the Spanish from the Indian districts and affords a splendid view of the Cerro Rico.

The Convento San Francisco, founded in 1547, is the oldest monastery in Bolivia. Its triple-nave basilica is adorned with several paintings by Pérez de Holguín. The crucified Christ on the main altar, El Señor de la Vera Cruz, is revered as the patron saint of the city.

The Plaza Murillo is the center of the Old City in La Paz; it was named after Bolivia's first freedom fighter, Pedro Domingo Murillo, who was executed here in 1810. Two statues on the square recall him as well as President Gualberto Villaroel, who was hanged in this spot in 1945. The Parliament building can be seen in the background (below). – The entrances to the Presidential Palace are flanked by a Guard of Honor (right).

Sucre – the Rebellious Beauty

The houses' red tiled roofs, window gratings and wooden balconies give the town an Andalusian flair. Founded in 1538 it was initially named Villa de la Plata, or La Plata ("Silver") for short. Since 1825 it has borne the name Antonio José de Sucre after the freedom fighter. Sucre is also known as Ciudad Blanca ("The White City") for its charming whitewashed façades. Built, like Rome, upon seven hills, Sucre became the capital of the newly founded state of Bolivia, but gradually, governmental functions transferred to La Paz; leaving only the Supreme Court in the original capital.

The Plaza 25 de Mayo, the city's main square, radiates something of the city's historical importance. This is the site of the Casa de la Libertad, built in 1621 as a Jesuit college with Mudéjar-style cloisters and a fountain in the central courtyard. From 1701 the building served as the San Francisco Javier University. It was here, on May 25, 1809, that the first Declaration of Independence in South America was signed, and it was in the Aula Magna (today the Salón de la Independencia) that Bolivia's independence was proclaimed on August 6, 1825. The blackish-brown spot which the agitated Simón Bolívar left on the tablecloth as he signed the Declaration of Independence is still visible today. On the walls hang portraits of freedom fighters Simón Bolívar, Antonio José de Sucre and Hugo Ballivián as well as documents and relics relating to the struggle for independence. In the middle of the room stands a huge bust of Bolívar weighing four tons – carved from the massive trunk of an algarrobo tree.

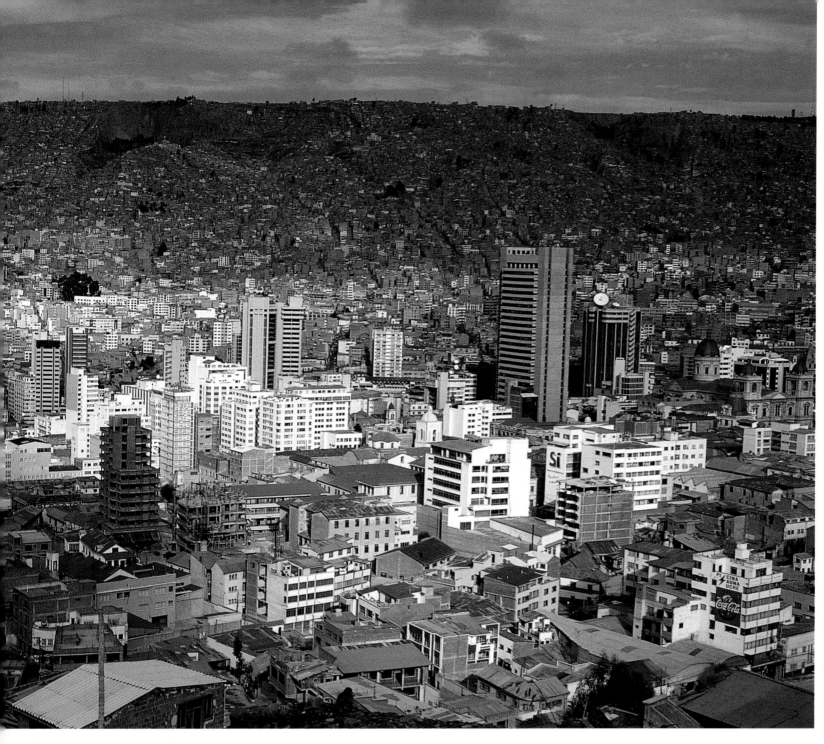

"The White Sea"

The Salar de Uyuni, a vast salt pan approximately 500 kilometers (313 miles) southwest of La Paz, extends over an area of 10,500 square kilometers (4,053 square miles) and is the largest area of salt in the world. The rocks and San Pedro cactuses of the Isla de los Pescadores (Fishermen's Island) rise like a phantom out of the glittering salt lake. On the edge of the "White Sea", as the locals call it, an extinct volcano, the Cerro Tunupa (5,432 meters/ 17,817 feet) towers up. You can climb to the summit from the village of Jiriri, where you will be rewarded by a magnificent view of the Altiplano landscape.

The dusty road runs straight as a die from the Salar de Uyuni towards San Juan, bordered by unpretentious low huts of adobe

La Paz, the unofficial capital of Bolivia, located in a protected basin at an altitude of about 3,700 meters (12,136 feet), makes it the world's highest metropolis (above). On the Avenida 16 de Julio, modern glass buildings tower behind the equestrian statue of the hero of the South American struggle for freedom, Simón Bolívar, who gave his name to the Republic of Bolivia, founded in 1825 (left).

See page 120   115

The Cañón del Huaricunca near La Paz.

Llama, Macaw, Andean Bear

The Fauna of Peru and Bolivia

1 The animal world of Peru is remarkable for its variety. The metallic shimmering blue morpho butterfly lives primarily in the rain forests 2 A falcon in the Cañón del Colca. 3 The llama is the best-known mammal in the Andes. It was domesticated many centuries ago and is used above all as a beast of burden. – 4 The spectacled bear (Andean bear) lives in the cloud forests of the eastern Andean cordillera. – 5 The wool of the wild vicuña is considered to be the finest in the world. – 6 The red-headed barbet has magnificent plumage. – 7 The plumage of the chaco pipit, which lives in the reeds of Lake Titicaca, is inconspicuous by comparison. – 8 In the Amazon region you can observe macaws in their natural habitat. – 9 Another native of the jungles of the Amazon region is the ocelot.

The Andes is the habitat for a wide range of fauna. The vicuña (*Lama vicugna*), for instance, a wild llama species related to the camel, lives here. The guanaco is another member of the same family; the domesticated llama and alpaca were both bred from these wild species. The coat of the vicuña is much sought-after as it makes for the finest wool in the world. Over the centuries of Spanish colonization, unscrupulous hunters decimated these dainty wild llamas, and their numbers fell to a dangerously low level. Today they are protected, and shearing them is only allowed in strictly limited circumstances.

You will be very lucky indeed if you see an Andean mountain cat (*Felis jacobita*); very little is known of its way of life. Its soft, thick fur provides good protection against the dry cold of its habitat. As well as lizards and birds it is thought to eat mountain viscachas and other small rodents.

Mountain viscachas are members of the chinchilla family. They are active during the daytime and feed on a wide variety of plants. These little animals leap and climb with great skill across even the steepest slopes, finding places to hide in caves and cracks in the rock.

The wild guinea pig (*Cavia aperea*) is another species of rodent. It is the species from which the domestic guinea pig evolved. For a long time it has been bred in the Andean Highlands by the Indígenas as a supply of meat; during the 16th cen-

siensis) lives on the rocky slopes of the Puna. In build it resembles the ibex, indicating that it is has remarkable agility for jumping from rock to rock. The taruca is extremely rare not only caused by its food supplies being reduced by

or Andean jackal (*Pseudalopex culpaeus*, previously *Dusicyon culpaeus*) is not at risk from extinction. The culpeo, which lives in the high plains of the Andes, prefers natural caves for its home or uses the sets of other animals.

bird in the world which can fly. It is classed among the New World vultures, although research indicates it has more genetic proximity to the stork. It circles for hours, over vast areas, in its search for carrion. Thermal currents permitting, it

9

can glide to heights of 8,000 meters (26,240 feet).

In the misty evergreen forests of the east, where the Andes cascade down towards the Amazon basin, live the woolly tapir, the puma and the spectacled bear (Andean bear), which plays an important role in the legends and myths of the Indígenas.

The variety of species living in the jungle regions of the Amazon is simply mind-boggling. At the tops of the enormous trees the ear-splitting screeches of monkeys and parrots echo while the undergrowth chirps with a myriad of insects. On the banks of the vast riverine labyrinth lurk caimans languidly waiting for their next victim, which include the equally feared piranha.

7

8

tury guinea pigs were first imported to Europe.

The North Andean deer or taruca (*Hippocamelus anti-*

domesticated animals and hunting, but also disease.

By contrast, the culpeo, also known as the Patagonian fox

The condor (*Vultur gryphus*) is the king of the Andes. Its wingspan of over three meters (10 feet) means it is the largest

119

The bizarre appearance of the Arbol de Piedra evidences how wind and weather have molded the rock over thousands of years (above). – The stony landscapes of the Bolivian Altiplano provide an ideal habitat for the cute viscacha (right).

bricks. Their roofs, penetrated by stove chimneys, are thatched with wild grass and the gables bear little wooden crosses or bull's horns to protect against evil spirits.

Enchanted lakes

On the Altiplano, 4,000 meters (13,120 feet) above sea level, south of San Juan are five lagoons (Conjunto de Lagunas): Laguna Cañapa with its white and yellow shores; Laguna Hedionda, at the foot of Caquella volcano (5, 947 meters/ 19,506 feet); Laguna Chiar Khota, meaning "Black Mud"; Laguna Honda; and Laguna Ramaditas, beneath the Cerro Ascotán (5,595 m/18,352 feet). The mineral-rich waters are the habitat for flocks of highland flamingos.

120

Across the 4,500 meter (14,760 feet) Paso de Inca is the Arbol de Piedra, a six-meter (20-foot) high rock so eroded by the wind it has the shape of a bizarre tree. Laguna Colorada affords the most spectacular view. Its high plankton content makes the lake, which spans an area of almost 60 square kilometers (23 square miles), appear red at its center. The clear water around its edges reflects the blue Andean sky, and here and there it is speckled with green algae and white islands of borax. But the dominant color is red and over the course of the day, as the sun moves across the sky, one can witness the entire range of red hues, from the palest pink to deep blood-red.

South of the Laguna Colorada, the traveler will find a bubbling "infernal spectacle": the Sol de Mañana geyser spews out hot water into the cold air, while all around mud pools bubble and steam hisses from narrow cracks in the earth. Not far away is the Laguna Verde with its fascinating display of color. Mornings see it an almost cloudy dark green, but as the sun rises the water surface changes to an intense, shimmering turquoise due to the high concentration of lead, sulphur and calcium carbonate. The Laguna Verde surpasses all the other lakes in its radiance, especially in the early morning, when the sun's rays strike the water surface at a slightly slanting angle. In the background the conical form of Mount Licancábur (5,930 meters/19,450 feet), one of the highest dormant volcanoes in the Andes which also marks the border with Chile casts its giant shadow. Centuries ago the Inca made sacrifices to the sun god Inti on its icy summit.

In Laguna Colorada a combination of micro organisms and mineral substances conjure up a bright palette of different colors in the barren landscape of the Bolivian Altiplano. Laguna Hedionda is also rich in minerals; it is here that the Andean flamingos gain sustenance (right).

With an area of 12,000 square kilometers (4,632 square miles) the Salar
de Uyuni in southwest Bolivia is one of the largest salt lakes in the world.

When Devils Dance

Festivals in Peru and Bolivia

1 and 6 The Corpus Christi festivities in Cuzco last for a whole week. Masked and costumed dancers perform in the city streets. 2 Another important spectacle is the festival in honor of Nuestro Señor Jesús de Gran Poder, held annually in May or June in La Paz. – 3 During the Corpus Christi procession in Cuzco a magnificently clad statue of Santa Rosa de Lima, the patron saint of soldiers, is carried around the Plaza de Armas. – 4 A good-natured group of dancers at a festival in Puno, the folklore capital of Peru. – 5 All in red: a participant in the Corpus Christi procession in Cuzco.

The Peruvian and Bolivian festivals are particular charming for the way they combine Christian elements with the ancient beliefs of the Indígenas.

One of the most important festivals in Cuzco is Inti Raymi, the ancient Inca festival marking the winter solstice. It is celebrated on June 23 and 24.

Colorful processions make their way through the streets. It climaxes with the arrival of the Inca at the historic ruins of Sacsayhuamán.

The five-day Qoyllur Riti festival is celebrated during the days before Corpus Christi in the Sinakara valley southeast of Cuzco, at a height of 4,600

meters (15,088 feet). Thousands of pilgrims arrive to climb one of the glaciers at the foot of the 6,336 meter (20,782 feet) high Auzangate. From here pieces of ice and huge blocks of ice are carried down into the valley, for the melted water is believed to have healing properties. The pilgrims

126

4

5

6

in Lima in honor of the city's patron saint, Santa Rosa de Lima (August 30). An important event in the Peruvian capital is also the festive procession in honor of El Señor de los Mila-gros ("The Lord of Miracles"), when hundreds of thousands of Christians dressed in purple form a procession behind an image of the Savior.

The colorful Fiesta de Nuestro Señor Jesús de Gran Poder is celebrated in La Paz in May or June with festive processions and dances.

are accompanied by dancers in brightly colored costumes and strange masks and village musicians.

Almost every town is famous for a particular festival. Thus the Festival of the Blessed Virgin of Copacabana (August 5 – 8) is one of the annual highlights alongside the procession

127

In the Heat of the Tropics

The Amazon Lowlands

The selva, the green rainforest to the east of the Andes, covers some 60 percent of the land area of Peru. The first European to travel along the full length of the Amazon as far as the mouth of the river was the Spanish conquistador Francisco de Orellana, in 1541/42. He was accompanied by the Dominican priest Gaspar Fray de Carvajal, who was ultimately responsible for naming the mighty river. Encountering a warlike tribe of women, the priest's classical education inspired him to compare them with the mythical Amazons of ancient Greek literature. And thus the expression "Río Amazonas" was born – although at first the river system was known as the Río Orellana after the man who first explored it.

The Spanish took almost nine months to reach the Atlantic, enduring great hardship along the way. For today's tourist the region is easier to explore. You can start your voyage through the green universe from of the numerous lodges near Iquitos, Pucallpa or Puerto Maldonado and return to base after just a few hours or days.

The variety of species of flowers and birds in the rain forests of the Amazon region is almost inexhaustible (top, bottom, right-hand page). – The Yagua Indians live near Iquitos on the banks of the world's greatest river (center).

Floating Houses and Jungle Steamers

Iquitos is Peru's gateway to the Atlantic, one of the most important Amazon ports in South America. The jungle city experienced its golden age during the rubber boom of the early 20th century.

128

An unusual way of going for a walk: the Amazon Canopy Walkway leads through the treetops of the giant evergreen trees (left).

The bars of Iquitos are a popular meeting place (above). The gray metal house, built by Gustave Eiffel, is a famous landmark. A wealthy rubber baron had it brought to Iquitos around 1890 (below).

Today it is an important trans-shipment location for the export of wood and oil. Several tens of thousands of the 400,000 inhabitants of Iquitos live in the Belén district, a shanty settlement on the banks of the Amazon. The houses are built on stilts or pontoons to cope with the water levels, which rise dramatically during the rainy season. When the river floods they look like houseboats in the water. Traders paddle their heavily laden boats along the canals between the houses.

Iquitos is probably the largest city in the world impossible to be reached by car, but only by boat or by air. It is an ideal point of departure for jungle tours, such as those by motor boat.

Pucallpa on the Río Ucayali, one of the twin sources of the Amazon, is a rapidly growing industrial city with oil refineries and factories. It has little to offer tourists – in contrast to the Laguna Yarinacocha, an idyllic lake only ten kilometers (6 miles) away, surrounded by tropical vegetation which forms the habitat of a varied range of animal species. Pleasure boats made expeditions to the villages of the Shipibo Indians on the shores of the lagoon.

The name of the town of Puerto Maldonado can be traced back to Faustino Maldonado. In the 19th century he was the first European to traverse the region from the West as far as the border with Brazil. A river steamer which ran aground in the jungle near Puerto Maldonado dating back to the turn of the last century, is thought to have belonged to the rubber baron Carlos Fer-

mín Fitzcarrald, who had the first steamship dragged eight kilometers (five miles) across the jungle from the upper reaches of the Río Mishagua to the Río Manú. The story became world famous in Werner Herzog's film Fitzcarraldo.

From the Yungas to the Llanos

An all-weather road runs from La Paz through the yungas via Caranavi and Yucumo to Rurrenabaque. The yungas occupy the transitional zone from the eastern slopes of the Cordillera Oriental to the Amazon Basin. Between 2,000 and 500 meters (6,560 –

The dugout canoe is still the traditional means of transport for the inhabitants of the Amazon region (above). The Yagua hunt monkeys and other small jungle animals with blowpipes and poisoned arrows (left).

131

Holiday in the Jungle

A stay in one of the many jungle lodges provides a good opportunity to get to know the Amazon rainforest of Peru. Motor boats transport you from Iquitos downstream to the comfortable, palm-thatched jungle accommodation such as the "Explorama Inn" and the "Jungle Amazon Inn".

More modestly equipped are the "Explorama Lodge" and the "ExplorNapo Lodge", from where you can walk through the tree tops of the giant jungle trees along the Amazon Canopy Walkway. If you travel downstream from Puerto Maldonado along the Río Madre de Díos you will come to the "Lago Sandoval Lodge", built of mahogany driftwood. The "Posada Amazonas" by the Río Tambopata lures visitors with excursions to observe the wildlife. The only lodge in the famous Manú National Park – die "Manú Lodge" – guarantees an unforgettable jungle experience.

Since the water level of the Amazon rises rapidly during the rainy season, the huts in Belén, a district of Iquitos, are built on stilts or pontoons (large photo); all aspects of everyday life take place on the river banks (right). – Siesta (above).

1,640 feet) gorges with luxuriant vegetation and dense, misty montane forests and a mild climate provide a foretaste of the tropical lowlands. This is the location of Rurrenabaque. The name of the tourist center of the Amazon rainforest is derived from the Tacana expression suse enabaque ("Duck Pond"). The picturesque jungle town is also known as La Perla del Beni.

The sand track heads from Yucumo in the direction of Trinidad towards San Ignacio de Moxos. The majority of the population is of the Indian Macheteros tribe. Founded in 1689 by Jesuit priests, the town had to be rebuilt in 1760 on higher, firmer ground. San Ignacio de Moxos is famous for its Easter festival and for its feast of Saint Ignatius Loyola on July 31st. The church on the Plaza 31 de Julio is 250 years old. It has pillars of almond wood and has lately been meticulously restored. The elongated roofs of the single-story houses also unmistakably register Jesuit design.

Nearby lie the Llanos de Moxos, an area of marshes and alluvial land of irrigation canals and embankments. It is regularly

flooded by the tributaries of the Río Mamoré during the rainy season. The bird population is exceptionally varied populated by blue-yellow macaws, black-headed storks, jaribus, cormorants, ibises, spoonbills, green parrots and the black-faced cotinga sporting its bright red and black plumage.

The Ai in the Public Garden

The little tropical town of Trinidad has a rather provincial air. Founded in the mid-16th century yet having virtually no tourist attractions of note, it is nonetheless a favorite starting point for river trips on the Río Mamoré.

Santa Cruz de la Sierra lies in the eastern lowlands of Bolivia, in the transition zone between the damp tropical north and the dry plains of the chaco. The fast-growing city has a population of almost one million, making it the most important metropolis in the country after La Paz.

Cure-all and Drug

The Coca Bush and Cocaine

At the place where the foothills of the Andes give way to the Amazon Basin, is the broad valley of the Río Huallaga, the main growing area for coca. The drugs trade blossoms here and conflict is rife between the drugs mafia, dealers, the drugs squad and the farmers who earn many times more by selling coca leaves than coffee or bananas. The Huallaga Valley produces more than one third of the world coca harvest.

The cultivation and consumption of coca leaves has a long tradition in Peru. It is likely that coca leaves were chewed as early 1000 BC by the Chavín culture; thanks to the stimulant and analgesic one becomes insensitive to cold and unaware of hunger or thirst. Tea made with coca leaves (mate de coca) counters the symptoms of *soroche*, altitude sickness.

The coca plant (erythroxylon coca) is a robust shrub which grows wild requiring virtually no care. The leaves can be harvested three to four times a year.

It is estimated that 70,000 hectares of land (172,900 acres) are planted with coca plants, supporting the poverty-stricken existence of some 80,000 peasants.

When the French chemist Angelo Mariani introduced a wine made with coca leaves, Vin Mariani, onto the European market in the mid-19th

7

8

1 A dignitary buys coca leaves (drawing from "El primer nueva crónica y buen gobierno" by Felipe Huamán Poma de Ayala). – 2 and 3 The coca plant is easy to cultivate and can be harvested several times a year. – 4 The drugs war: in the struggle against the cocaine cartels even the army is involved. 5 The cultivation and consumption of coca leaves in Peru is based on a thousand-year-old tradition. 6 Cocaine being enjoyed in a cheerful round. – 7 The miners in Bolivia chew coca leaves to help endure the harsh working conditions. – 8 Religious sacrifice.

6

century, it soon became popular. American soft-drink manufacturers followed suit with their own products based on coca – such as Coca-Cola.

Cocaine was isolated from coca leaves for the first time in 1860 by the chemist Albert Niemann. To produce the narcotic, the leaves are processed

locally together with various chemicals to form a dry paste which is then further processed in the jungle laboratories of Colombia to produce cocaine hydrochloride – the white powder inhaled as a recreational drug in industrial countries. The harvest of a one-hectare (2.47 acre) coca field will produce between four and four and a half kilos of cocaine. Peru and Bolivia are two of the principal coca-producing countries. Cocaine production and the drugs trade, by contrast, are firmly in the hands of the powerful Colombian drug cartels.

135

The Amazon region occupies more than half of the land area of Peru, but only five percent of the population lives here (right and top). The church of Concepción is one of the loveliest Jesuit missions in Bolivia (below).

In the Care of the Jesuits

The Plaza 24 de Septiembre at the city center is planted with flowers, palm trees and ambaibo trees, where large numbers of wild sloths have taken up residence. The square is bordered by numerous cafés, restaurants, various banks, a cinema, the Town Hall and the prefecture of the province of the same name. On the south side, next to the prefecture building, the massive silhouette of the Basilica Menor de San Lorenzo is unavoidable.

Between 1692 and 1760 ten missionary villages were established in the Llanos de Chiquitos following the pattern devised by the Dominican priest Bartolomé de las Casas, who, between 1515 and 1522, built the first villages intended exclusively for Indians in Venezuela. Between 2,000 and 3,000 Guarani or Chiquito Indians lived in a sort of rural community, in what are called reductions, each of which are run by two Jesuit priests.

136

Six of the especially well preserved Jesuit reductions were included in the UNESCO World Cultural Heritage list in 1990 for their architectural structure and have been scrupulously restored over recent years: San Francisco Javier, Concepción, Santa Ana, San Miguel, San Rafael and San José de Chiquitos.

San Francisco Javier, the first mission station, was founded at the end of 1691. Of particular note is the church, built between 1749 and 1752 by the Swiss Jesuit priest Martin Schmid; the carved wooden pillars and ornamentation, paintings and wall

The mighty Basilica Menor de San Lorenzo (1845 to 1915) in Santa Cruz (Bolivia) with its three naves in the Jesuit style has a high altar with precious silver decorations. The figures of the crucified Christ (17th century) are of ivory.

decorations are complemented by a very fine baptistery with a wooden font.

The church of Concepción is particularly distinguished, the wooden building features a main nave and two side aisles in which six rows of pillars bear the roof. It was completed in 1755 and completely restored between 1975 and 1982. The church has three altars; the central altar (La Astuta) is dedicated to the Virgin Mary, carved from cedar wood and decorated with gold leaf.

Today San Ignacio de Velasco, the center of the Chiquitos reduction, has a population of 14,000. This was once the site of the largest mission church, almost entirely wooden. But in 1974 it was demolished and replaced by a new building.

San Miguel de Velasco is probably one of the prettiest mission stations. An attractively painted façade adorns the church and its old adobe bell tower, founded in 1721. Exceptional for its main altar, richly decorated with gold leaf and the luxuriant Baroque-inspired painted flower and shell decorations in the chancel. Carved wooden columns wind their way up to the ceil-

While the treetops are exposed to the sun and wind (above), virtually nothing penetrates down to the jungle floor below (below).

ing, adorned with a bright red heart. The sacristy bears a red sun with the inscription IHS, the insignia of the Jesuit order.

The church of San Rafael de Velasco, founded in 1696, also has a fine interior decoration. The colonnades and columns are of wood and the altar is covered in gold leaf, while the pulpit is adorned with glittering mica.

The reduction Santa Ana de Velasco has the plainest church building. The floor of the building, almost 250 years old, is of tamped clay; the palm-frond roof was only replaced with tiles in the 19th century. Between 1999 and 2000 the valuable wooden carvings in the interior were meticulously restored.

San José de Chiquitos was founded in 1698 as the third Jesuit mission station in the llanos. The solid-looking church complex was built entirely of stone; it consists of the confirmation chapel, the main church and the convent, in the inner courtyard of which there is a sundial without a pointer – here, far from the big-city bustle, time is of no significance in the Andes states.

The roots of the giant trees spread out several meters across the jungle floor (top left).
In the calmer waters of the Amazon, huge water lilies carpet its surface (bottom left).

139

The Amazon near Iquitos.

Mountain Mines, Rubber Boom

The Tin and Rubber Barons

1 Advertisement for rubber heels (c. 1910). – 2 The German scientist Alexander von Humboldt and his French colleague Aimé Bonpland carried out the first experiments on rubber trees on the Orinoco in 1799/1800 (painting by Eduard Ender, 19th century). 3 In the mines of Bolivia, mining techniques have hardly changed over the past 450 years. 4 Charles Goodyear developed the process of vulcanization in 1839 in den United States. Raw rubber is treated with sulfur to produce rubber. – 5 and 6 The veterinary surgeon John Boyd Dunlop invented the air-filled rubber tire in 1888.

Simón Iturbi Patino was born in 1860 in a little village south of Cochabamba. He served an apprenticeship at a firm which sold mining equipment. Among the customers was the owner of a tin mine in Oruro who had got into economic difficulties. In 1897 Patino bought the mountain mine for a song. Three years later the vein of tin they had discovered became one of the most profitable in the world. Patino's tin empire expanded as far as Asia, Africa and Oceania. He moved his company headquarters to the United States and settled in Paris.

During 1915 - 1927 he built the Palacio de los Portales in

8

Cochabamba along the lines of Versailles, but never actually lived in it. Nor did he ever live in the home he planned to retire to, the magnificent Villa Albina near Cochabamba, death caught up with Patino in Buenos Aires at the age of 86.

Immense wealth was also the reward for those aware of how to profit from rubber, the "White

7

Gold" of the Amazon region. The invention of the pneumatic tire in particular led to an enormous demand for rubber, sparking off a rubber boom in the rainforest in around 1900. The boom was over as quickly as it had begun. Asia entered the world market with its rubber produce and by 1911 a glut collapsed the entire market.

Nonetheless, in 1912 a railroad was inaugurated between Guayaramirim in Bolivia and Porto Velho in Brazil; the rubber barons Nicolás Suárez and Julio César Arana had both invested enormous sums in its construction. The route had been intended to provide Riberalta, the center of rubber production, with access to the Atlantic. The laying of rails through the jungle, which cost the lives of countless workers, turned out to be a waste of money. The final section to Riberalta was never completed – Suárez and Arana had completely miscalculated. Today the engines rust on; forgotten in the Brazilian jungle.

Together with his brothers and the rubber pioneer Vaca Diez, Nicolás Suárez had founded "The Orton Rubber Company". After the death of Vaca Diez, Suárez continued to expand his company fortune. He became the richest man in the Amazon region; the towns of Riberalta and Villabella numbered among his many properties. His son-in-law Napoléon, inherited the company in 1940 and, with his wife, squandered the entire fortune in a just few years.

143

Planning your Journey

Size/Location/ Topography

Peru (1,285,216 square kilometers/ 496,093 square miles) lies between the Equator and 18°20' south and between 69° and 82° west. Bolivia (1,098,581 square kilometers/ 424,052 square miles) lies between 58° and 69° west and between 10° and 23° south. Peru is characterized by three distinct geographical regions distinctly separate from one another: the coastal plain (Costa), the highlands (Sierra) and the plains in the east, which are mainly covered in rain

two chains by the valley of the Río Santa (also known as the Callejón de Huaylas): the western Cordillera Negra and the Cordillera Blanca, which rises up to the east of the valley. The Eastern Cordillera, by contrast, does not extend northwards and southwards as a continuous chain, but is interrupted by major rivers (Río Apurimac, Río Urubamba). Both mountain ranges join together further south to form the Cordillera Huayhuash. In Southern Peru and especially in Bolivia the Andes, now divided again into a Western, Eastern and Central Cordillera, gradually attain their maximum width. Between

Threatened with extinction: the giant bromeliad.

south (Salar de Uyuni). The coastal zone extends for 2,300 kilometers (1,438 miles) along the Pacific Ocean. Some areas are such barren they count amongst the driest regions in the country. Eastern Pe-

ru features the vast lowlands and the Amazon region. In Bolivia the eastern slopes of the Eastern Cordillera are called the Yungas; the deeply eroded valley of Cochabamba, Sucre and Tarija are known as Valles. In the northern section of the East (Oriente) the Amazon region of damp lowland rainforest gives way further south to the flood plains of the savannah wetlands (Llanos) and the grasslands of the Pampas.

Flora and Fauna

The Andes shape a clear line of demarcation between the climate of the dry Pacific coastal region and the tropical lowlands of the

In the Urubamba Valley with the Cordillera de Vilcanota di andenes.

forest (Selva). In the highlands the Western and Eastern Cordilleras of the Andes run parallel to each other. The Western Cordillera (Cordillera Occidental) covers a wide area which extends down into southern Peru. It is split into

the Cordillera Central and the Cordillera Oriental are the wide expanses of the Altiplano and the Puna. At 3,000 meters (9,840 feet) above sea level, the high plateau is not fed by any rivers and proceeds to acquire a desert character in the

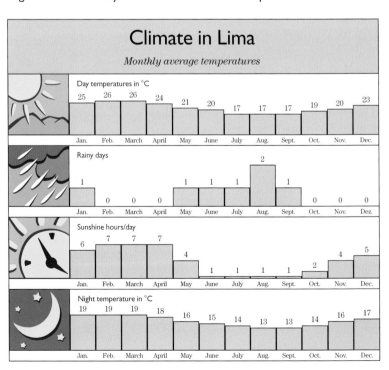

Climate in Lima
Monthly average temperatures

Day temperatures in °C											
25	26	26	24	21	20	17	17	17	19	20	23
Jan.	Feb.	March	April	May	June	July	Aug.	Sept.	Oct.	Nov.	Dec.

Rainy days											
1	0	0	0	1	1	1	2	1	0	0	0
Jan.	Feb.	March	April	May	June	July	Aug.	Sept.	Oct.	Nov.	Dez.

Sunshine hours/day											
6	7	7	7	4	1	1	1	1	2	4	5
Jan.	Feb.	March	April	May	June	July	Aug.	Sept.	Oct.	Nov.	Dec.

Night temperature in °C											
19	19	19	18	16	15	14	13	13	14	16	17
Jan.	Feb.	March	April	May	June	July	Aug.	Sept.	Oct.	Nov.	Dec.

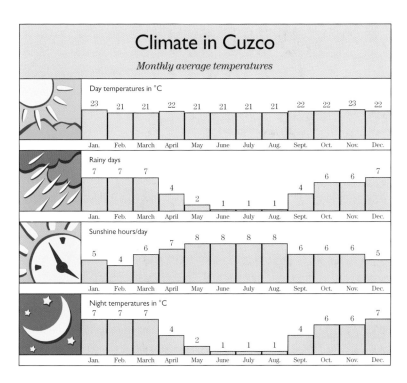

Climate in Cuzco
Monthly average temperatures

Day temperatures in °C	Jan.	Feb.	March	April	May	June	July	Aug.	Sept.	Oct.	Nov.	Dec.
	23	21	21	22	21	21	21	21	22	22	23	22

Rainy days	Jan.	Feb.	March	April	May	June	July	Aug.	Sept.	Oct.	Nov.	Dec.
	7	7	7	4	2	1	1	1	4	6	6	7

Sunshine hours/day	Jan.	Feb.	March	April	May	June	July	Aug.	Sept.	Oct.	Nov.	Dec.
	5	4	6	7	8	8	8	8	6	6	6	5

Night temperatures in °C	Jan.	Feb.	March	April	May	June	July	Aug.	Sept.	Oct.	Nov.	Dec.
	7	7	7	4	2	1	1	1	4	6	6	7

Amazon. In the coastal region, on the western slopes of the Cordillera, where the Humboldt Current flows further away from the coast, the flora is largely made up of green plants and shrubs for the regions are prone to fog (garúa). The most important plants are the carob (algarroba) and the rosé pepper tree.

Between 2,700 and 3,200 meters

Rice is grown in Northern Peru.

above sea level (8,856-10,496 feet) the vegetation is characterized by tough, resilient grasses, herbs and the odd shrub. In Northern Peru the bush land gives way to the tussock-grass steppes of the Puna,

which extend up to an altitude of 4,500 meters (14,760 feet). The word puna (dream) refers to the heady sensations experienced as one ascends from the plains and the first symptoms of altitude sickness (soroche) make their mark. Typical plants in the Puna are the many species of rosette and cushion plants (for example llareta cushions), which are dried in the sun and used for fuel. Also characteristic of the Puna are the ichú tufted grasses.

The semi-desert regions of the Puna in Southern Bolivia give way to the Puna vegetation of the Atacama Desert in Northern Chile. At medium altitudes (2,000–3,800 m/6,560-12,464 ft) the upper eastern slopes of the Andes are covered by an evergreen cloud forest which is rich in species. This densely forested region of the tropical Andes is known in Peru as La Montaña; in Bolivia the mountain and cloud forests are known as

Yungas (near La Paz) or Valles (near Cochabamba). Tropical rain forest grows on the slopes at altitudes below 2,000 meters (6,560 feet). The floor of the Amazon rain forest is covered with foliage, uprooted tree trunks and luxuriant ferns. Above these rise palm trees and other trees, which again are surmounted by the lofty crowns of the giant forest trees. Countless orchids, bromeliads, creepers, heliconia, water plants, elephant grass, bamboo, hardwoods and the rubber and cinchona trees grow in

Wearing traditional dress: a woman in Chivay.

abundance in the flatlands of the Amazon jungle. Regions of savanna grassland (Llanos and Pampas) intersperse the expanse of tropical rain forest.

Population

Today the population of Peru is approximately 27.5 million, Bolivia around 8.7 million. Both countries are characterized by a high percentage of Indígenas. In Bolivia they total more than 55 percent of the population and in Peru 45 percent. In Peru there are also a large number of mestizos (37 percent). Peruvians of mixed race, combining both Criollo (descendants of the Spanish who were born in the New World) and Indígena blood are also known as Cholos. In Bolivia 35 percent of the population is of mixed race. The remaining minority are Europeans, Africans, Asians (especially Chinese and Japanese) and Arabs. The small, wealthy, white upper class forms a self-contained society. The population is growing rapidly in both coun-

The Fiesta Nuestro Señor Jesús de Gran Poder in La Paz is as colorful as it is spectacular.

A traditional dance in the fields: in November the arrival of the first Inca is celebrated in Puno.

tries. Bolivia has an annual growth rate of 2.33 percent and Peru of 1.73 percent. Population density in Peru is 19.3 inhabitants per square kilometer (50 per square mile); in Bolivia only 7.2 inhabitants per square kilometer (19 per square mile). The overwhelming majority of the inhabitants live in the cities (72 percent in Peru, 68 percent in Bolivia). Most Indígenas, however, live in the Andes Highlands. A number of small Indian tribes live in the Amazon jungle.

Language

The national language is Spanish; the Indígenas also speak Aymará (in the region around Lake Titicaca and in Bolivia) and Quechua, the language of the Incas.

Best Time to Visit

Best time to visit the highlands is during the sunny months between June and the beginning of September, when, however, it can be extremely cold at night. The best season to travel to Lima, which suffers badly from the *garúa*, is between September and November and from March to May. The recommended season for the Eastern Lowlands and the Amazon region is the period between the end of May and July.

Time Zones

New York: Peru – no time difference, La Paz plus 1 hour. London: Peru minus 5 hours, Bolivia minus 4 hours.

Festivals/Public Holidays

In addition to Easter, Christmas, New Year, All Saints' Day (Día de Todos los Santos) and various local holidays as well as May 1 (Día de los Trabajadores/ Labor Day), a number of national holidays are also celebrated.
In Peru:
June 14: Día de los Campesinos (Farmers' Day)
June 29: Fiesta de San Pedro y San Paulo (SS. Peter and Paul)
July 28/29: Día de Independencia

(Independence Day)
August 15: Virgen de la Asunción (Assumption of the Virgin Mary)
August 30: Santa Rosa de Lima (Festival of the patron saint of Lima)
October 9: Día de la Dignidad Nacional (Day of National Dignity)
In Bolivia:
August 6: Día de Independencia (Independence Day)

Arrival

The main airport in Peru is J. Chavez International in Lima. Direct flights between the United States and Lima take some 8 to 10 hours; flight times between London and Lima take 14 to 15 hours; between Canada and the capital of Peru 11 to 13 hours. Bolivia's principal airport in La Paz can be reached directly from New York in 10 to 18 hours; from London the flight will take approx. 19.5 hours. The airport charge for international flights in Bolivia and Peru is 25 US-$ per flight.

Medical Facilities

Hospitals which can be visited in an emergency are only found in major cities. All doctor's bills must be paid immediately in cash. There are very few dentists. In an emergency, your embassy will be able to provide the address of a doctor.

Information

Peruvian Embassy
United Kingdom: Embajada del Perú en el Reino Unido de Gran

Bretaña e Irland del Norte, London
52 Sloane Street, London SW1X 9SP, UK, Tel. +44 (020) 7235 1917, 7235 8340, 7235 3802
Australia: Embajada del Perú en Australia, Canberra

Cuzco: on the Plaza de Armas (above), arcades (right) and an inner courtyard (far right).

Typical regional headgear

40 Brisbane Avenue, Piso 2 Barton, 2606 ACT, Canberra, Australia, Tel. + 61 (2) 6290 0959
embassy@embaperu.org.au
USA: Embajada del Perú en los Estados Unidos de América, Washington, D.C.
1700 Massachusetts Ave. N.W. Washington D.C. 20036
Tel. +1 (202) 363 4808, 363 4809, comunica@embassyofperu.us

The Inca City

A Stroll through Cuzco

The starting point for a stroll through Cuzco is the Plaza de Armas. Dominating the square is the mighty cathedral, which occupies the very site where once the palace of the Inca Viracocha stood. Immediately to the right of the cathedral is the church of El Triunfo – so named for the victory of the Spanish over the Inca under Manco Cápac II in 1536. This was also the location of Suntur Huasi, the Inca's most important armorer. Even the Jesuit church La Compañia diagonally opposite is built, like so many colonial buildings in Cuzco, on the foundations of an Inca palace. The narrow Calle Loreto leads to the remains of Coricancha, the famous Temple of the Sun and the most sacred Inca site, above which the conquistadors built the Monastery of Santo

Domingo. If you now turn back towards the Plaza de Armas, you will pass the Museo Santa Catalina on your way to the most interesting street in town, the Calle Hatun Rumiyoc. The most famous sight here is the twelve-sided stone which was part of the exterior wall of the Palace of the Inca Roca. Today it is the site of the Museo de Arte Religioso.

Despite its nondescript appearance, the Iglesia de San Blas – which was badly damaged during the earthquakes of 1650 and 1950 – still retains its beautifully carved altars and large-format paintings by artists of the Cuzco School. Passing the Convent of the Nazarenes and the Iglesia San Antonio Abad, the narrow "Alley of the Seven Serpents" (Calle

de Siete Culebras) leads past the corner of Tucumán/Ataud to the Inca Museum. Its collection of Inca artifacts is worth a visit.

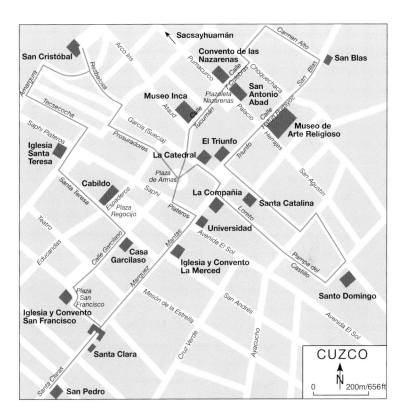

Returning to the Plaza de Armas, we now proceed along the Calle Mantas passing the University of Cuzco on our way to the monastery church of La Merced, the oldest church in Cuzco. The cobbled road now leads gently uphill towards the Plaza San Francisco. Passing through an old archway the Church of Santa Clara is to be seen, with its fine mirrored altars, before reaching the Baroque Church of San Pedro. On the way back, skirting round the Plaza San Francisco, we pass the monastery church of the same name, which houses a monumental painting of St. Francis, and then follow the Calle Garcilaso to the Casa de Garcilaso, the birthplace of the chronicler.

Arriving at the Plaza Regocijo (Square of Rejoicing), we are now facing the old Town Hall (Cabildo), which is now an art museum. The Calle Santa Teresa leads on to the Iglesia Santa Teresa, also built on ancient Inca walls. The tour continues as far as the Iglesia San Cristóbal, built on the site of the palace (Colcampata) of Manco Cápac, before we wind up once more at the Plaza de Armas.

147

Canada: Embajada del Perú en
Canada, Ottawa
130 Albert Street, Suite 1901,
Ottawa, Ontario (Canadá) K1P 5G4
Tel. +1 (613) 722 6042
emperuca@bellnet.ca
Telephone information/ assistance
in planning a trip:
PERU: PromPerú (Commission
for the Promotion of Peru)

Currency

The national currency of Peru is
the Nuevo Sol = 100 Céntimos
(Sol); in Bolivia it is the Boliviano =
100 Centavos.
1 Euro = 4.25 Sol, 1 US$ = 3.21 Sol,
1 £ Sterling = 6.31 Sol, 1 Canad.$
= 2.98 Sol, 1 Austr.$ = 2.67 Sol.
1 Euro = 10.78 Boliviano, 1 US-$ =

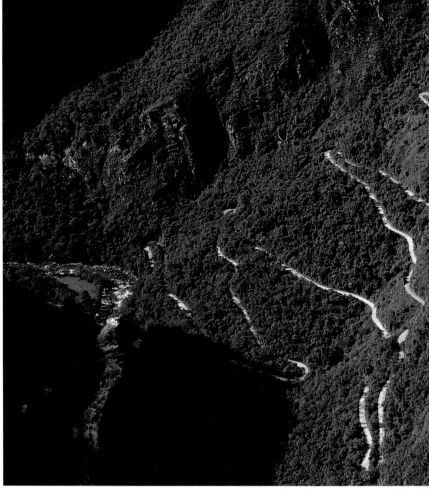

The "Peru Rail" runs from Cuzco to Machu
Picchu (above). – View from the Huayna Picchu
into the Urubamba Valley (right).

Calle 1 Oeste 50,
Edificio Mincetur, 13th Floor,
Urb. Córpac, San Isidro, PE-Lima 27
Tel: +51 (01) 224 31 31.
Fax: (01) 225 11 63.
postmaster@promperu.gob.pe
http://www.promperu.gob.pe

Visas

Citizens of Australia, the United Kingdom, Ireland, and Canada require a
passport which is valid for at least six
months. A visa is not required for a
stay of less than three months. Citizens of the United States have required a visa since January 2007.

Giant sand dunes rise up along the coast in southern Peru.

7.89 Boliviano, 1 Pound Sterling =
15.90 Boliviano, 1 Canad.$ = 7.51
Boliviano, 1 Austr.$ = 6.55 Boliviano.

Banks

In Peru money can be changed in
banks, bureaux de change, hotels

and by street traders with a
license.
In Bolivia the bureaux de change
(Casas de cambios) are mostly rep-
utable and give a good exchange
rate.
In both countries traveler's checks
in US-$ are not always accepted.

Credit cards are widely used, but
are not accepted at gas stations.
Peru: open Monday–Friday 9
a.m.–12 noon, 2–4 p.m., however
there may be regional differences.

Shopping

Bolivia: open Monday–Friday 9
a.m. –12, 2.30–5.30 p.m.
In both Peru and Bolivia the traveler will find a wide range of souvenirs, but the quality of the
goods on offer may vary widely
depending on the region. The
same applies to prices. Bargaining
is essential.
Peru: Shops and supermarkets are
open from Monday to Saturday
between 9 a.m. and 1 p.m. and
from 3–7 p.m.

Surfing on the reed "ponies": fishermen on the coast near Huanchaco.

Bolivia: There are no fixed opening hours. In larger cities most shops are open from Monday to Friday between 9 a.m. and 1 p.m. and between 3–7 p.m. On Saturdays they are mostly open from 10 a.m.–1 p.m.

Electricity

In Peru, the electricity voltage in the main cities is 220V. Larger hotels have 110V power sockets for electric shavers in the bathrooms. In Bolivia the voltage is generally 220V; in La Paz it is 110V. Adapters for US flat sockets are required.

Getting around

Car: The least expensive arrangement is to reserve a rental car

Traveling with Don José: a mooring in the jungle city of Iquitos.

with one of the international car hire firms before leaving home. All countries in the Andes require a valid national and international driving license with a photo as well as a credit card. Drivers must be at least 21 (or 25) years of age. Luxury coaches: Various private companies operate between the main cities. Coaches depart from the main bus stations (Terminal de Buses/Terrestre). The number of passengers is limited by the number of seats available, so it is advisable to make a reservation at the relevant bus station in good time.

Rail: The railroad network in Peru is small and in principle consists only of the stretch between Arequipa and Juliaca. The rail journey between Puno-Cuzco and Cuzco-Machu Picchu is very picturesque. It is advisable to make a reservation. The second-highest railroad in the world runs from Lima to Cerro de Pasco or Huancayo, reaching its highest point at La Cima (4,835m/ 15,859 ft). Tourist excursions with this "Tren Macho" take place from time to time. In Bolivia the railroad journey from Oruro to Uyuni is interesting.

Photography

There are virtually no legal restrictions on taking photographs with the exception of frontier and military complexes. In general, one should ask for permission before photographing people, especially Indígenas. Fees are often charged for using a video camera.

Health Precautions

Visitors arriving directly from Europe currently do not need any special vaccinations. A yellow fever vaccination is only required for visitors arriving from areas where yellow fever is endemic. It is recommended, however – as is malaria prophylaxis – for visitors traveling to the Amazon region.

149

Doctors' bills and prescriptions must be paid immediately in cash. In the High Andes visitors may suffer from the dreaded altitude sickness (*soroche*).

Mail is usually delivered to a post-office box, so it is necessary also to quote the post-office box (*casilla*) when listing one's address. The first name should never be

Traveling with children

A journey to Peru and Bolivia with small children is not recommended. The long flight from Europe or North America is exhausting, and furthermore conditions in the country itself are often far from comfortable. The food is frequently very fatty and highly spiced, and the high altitude may also prove especially problematic for children.

Postal Services

There are no postboxes or postmen, so all mail must be handed in directly at the post office (*correo*).

written out in full, since letters are stored alphabetically according to family name and to do so could lead to confusion between first and family names.

Valuable items are best sent by courier or international air freight. Packets must be cleared through customs.

The opening times of post offices in Peru:
generally Monday to Saturday 8 a.m. to 8 p.m.;
in Bolivia: Monday to Friday 8 a.m. to 8 p.m.

Souvenirs

In specialist shops in towns and on the market in the villages you will

Wall motifs in Túcume (left). – The library of the Monastery of San Francisco in Lima houses valuable treasures (above). – Woven belt from Taquile (top right). – On horseback (below right). – A herd of llamas (bottom right).

find a wide range of handicrafts which make suitable souvenirs. Vessels from Pre-Columbian times known as huacos are extremely expensive and the export of them is strictly forbidden. All such items on offer are almost certainly fakes. Otherwise you will also find a wide selection of ceramic goods, leather wares, ornately carved

with Micropur tablets or a Katadyn filter. Salt tablets and drinking regularly (more than is required to quench your thirst) are vitally important if walking fast enough to sweat. The intense solar radiation means good suntan cream and sunglasses are compulsory for adequate protection against UV rays. The temperature differences between day and night are extreme.

colonial-style wooden frames with inlaid mirrors and bronze imitations of gold leaf, as well as flowers made from the feathers of exotic birds and music cassettes with Peruvian folk music.

The woolen items are particularly attractive, since the alpacas supply silky-soft wool for pullovers, jackets, and ponchos, which could come in handy when visiting the chilly highlands making them very popular souvenirs.

Brightly woven cloth, knitted caps and mantas (shawls) as well as brightly woven goods, slippers, and bedspreads are also popular. The

best places to buy them are in Cuzco and by Lake Titicaca, but you will also find plenty of woolen items around Huaraz. In addition to textiles you will also find silver and gold jewelry decorated with historic patterns and motifs. The jewelry from the Trujillo region is particularly fine.

Sports/Trekking

In contrast to mountaineering, trekking requires no special technical skills. Most treks in the Peruvian Andes are not much more than extended walks, albeit along very

steep paths. Nonetheless, a number of rules should be observed. Most routes are at altitudes between 3,000 and 5,000 meters (9,840-16,400 feet). It is essential to become acclimatized before embarking on such a trek, for the body needs a certain amount of time to produce sufficient red blood corpuscles. Without this period of adjustment the thin air at these high altitudes will cause altitude sickness (headache, nausea, shortness of breath, sleeplessness). The snow line is at 4,800 meters (15,744 feet).

Drinking water should be treated

During the day it can be 18 to 20 degrees Celsius (64-68o Fahrenheit), but at night the temperature can drop to below freezing. Light thermal underwear, warm clothing and a down anorak are essential. You should inquire about the exact length of the trekking tour. Considerable differences in altitude and your luggage will significantly slow your progress. One should remember that near the Equator, day and night are of around the same duration – night falls at around 6 p.m. and lasts for 12 hours. You should have reached your goal by then at the latest.

See page 154 151

Discovering the Andes

The Five Most Picturesque Routes through Peru and Bolivia

Route 1: The coastal route

From the capital Lima the Panamericana highway runs both northward and southward along the coast. Along the Chimbote-Trujillo-Chiclayo-Lambayeque section is a succession of fascinating pre-Inca ruins. You can also visit Trujillo, the "City of Springtime", and view its fine

The volcano Misti, towering above the town of Arequipa, has been dormant for 130 years.

colonial buildings. Heading south the route passes the ruins of Pachacamac and the little town of Pisco on its way to the Bay of Paracas, where you can take a boat trip to the wildlife sanctuaries on the Islas Ballestas. The next highlight is provided by the spectacular geoglyphs in the desert around Nazca. The coastal route ends inland at Arequipa, the pearl of colonial Peru. From here an excursion takes you to the Cañón del Colca, to end a

largely cultural trip with a natural scenic highlight.

Route 2: The Andes route

This route begins in Cuzco, the former heart of the Inca Empire, and leads first of all to Machu Picchu, an essential element in any journey through South America. It then continues to Puno, the capital of

folklore on Lake Titicaca. From here a road leads along the western lakeshore across the Bolivian border to the pilgrimage town of Copacabana, to the Islands of the Sun and the Moon and to the ruins of Tiahuanaco. And finally La Paz, the highest metropolis in the world, will literally take your breath away.

Route 3: The mountain route

One of the most dramatic tours through the Andes is the trip to

"Peruvian Switzerland". The approach route follows the Panamericana highway in a northerly direction from Lima, passing through the towns of Huaura and Pativilca. Inland from the coast the road climbs steeply to an altitude of 4,080 meters (13,382 feet) at the Conococha Pass. Rendering grandiose views across the Cordillera Blanca it continues through the green high valley of the Callejón de Huaylas to Huaraz. Before you reach the mountaineering mecca you could make a detour to the ruins of Chavín de Huántar. From Huaraz the route leads to Yungay and Caraz (both offering trekking opportunities) through the precipitous Cañón del Pato as

Majestic: the Huascarán.

far as Huallanca, from where you can return to the coast.

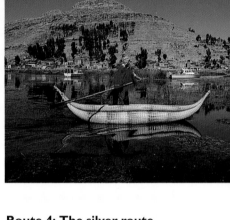

Route 4: The silver route

From La Paz the route follows the old silver trail of the Inca and the Spanish conquistadors to the pretty colonial town of Sucre and then on to Potosí. Passing through Uyuni you will reach the vast salt pans of the Salar de Uyuni, from where you can only continue in a jeep. The "Lagoon Road" offers a succession of unique scenic impressions with deep blue, black, red and blue-green lakes at the foot of snow-capped volcanoes as well as a desert with magnificent color effects and spouting geysers. Bizarre rock formations and little villages of crooked thatch-roofed cottages nestled in the wild grasses line the route to the Chilean border.

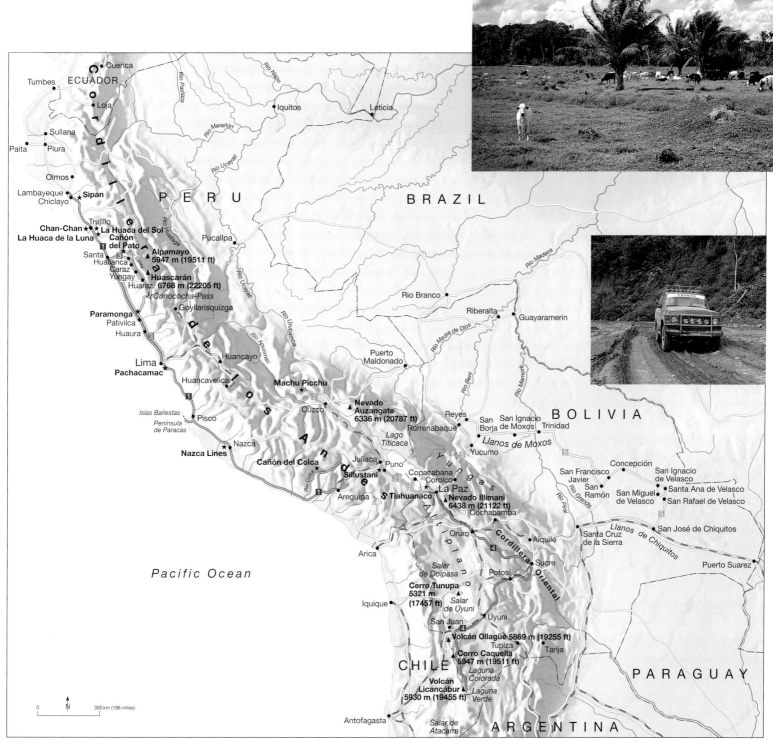

Route 5: The explorers' route

This long route through the lowlands of Bolivia is to be recommended for travelers blessed with a spirit of adventure and enough time to indulge it. Going from La Paz to Santa Cruz de la Sierra, it is just as fascinating taken from the opposite direction. The road from La Paz winds in endless hairpin bends through the Yungas down to

Sucre is the most attractive town in Bolivia.

Coroíco and continues past Yucumo on a bumpy track to Rurrenabaque, the "Pearl on the Río Beni". Passing through Reyes and San Borja you eventually reach the world of the Llanos and their vast cattle farms. Passing San Ignacio de Moxos you then continue to the tropical town of Trinidad. The section heading southeast to San Ramón seems endless, but the

tiring journey is worthwhile: the magnificently restored churches of the Jesuit missions of San Francisco Javier, Concepción, San Ignacio de Velasco, Santa Ana, San Rafael and San Miguel offer the visitor aesthetic delights. After a stopover in San José de Chiquitos the "Explorers' Route" ends in Santa Cruz de la Sierra, the second-largest city in Bolivia.

153

At 6,542 meters (21,458 feet) the Nevado Sajama in the Sajama National Park is the highest mountain in Bolivia and one of the tallest volcanoes in the world (large photo). Stone condors adorn a hotel near Puno (above). This hotel in San Ignacio de Velasco promises a relaxing stay (bottom).

Swimming

Although you can bathe on the Pacific beaches (especially near Lima and Trujillo), for hygienic reasons the opportunities are somewhat limited.

Telephones

In Peru and Bolivia the telephone network (voice calls and fax) has been run by the privatized company ENTEL since the end of 1994. Telephone cards are available in Peru from Telefónica del Perú, the largest telephone company, and elsewhere. Depending on your mobile phone provider you may be able to make calls using a triband phone. The international country code for Bolivia is 00591; for Peru it is 0051.

Tipping

In the more expensive restaurants and hotels, the service charge (servicio) and tip (propina) are included in the bill. Otherwise it is customary to give a ten percent tip for good service. If you go on an excursion the driver, guide, porter and cook will also expect a tip.

Accommodation

There is a wide range of hotels and hostels available in Peru. Major cities feature comfortable hotels of international standard, as well as good hotels and hostales. The difference lies in the number of rooms, not in the quality (a hostal has no more than 50 rooms).

Accommodation for all price brackets: rough-ing it in a tent (top left); in the rustic tourist complex of Landhaus Samaipata at the eastern foothills of the Bolivian Andes (left); or in the luxury hotel Bolívar in Lima (far left).

Bolivia: In the larger cities you will find, in addition to a number of good hotels and hostales (sometimes in lovely colonial buildings), unpretentious residenciales and alo-jamientos, in which there is usually no heating and often no guarantee of hot water.

There are no youth hostels in either country.

Customs

Customs controls for normal groups and individual travelers are usually carried out with a degree of tolerance. Drugs, however, are forbidden and carry severe penalties. Endangered species and antiques are subject to an export ban. Items for personal use may be imported duty-free (please inquire).

155

People, Places, General Expressions

Figures in *italics* refer to photos; colored squares and figures in **bold type** to specials; colored headings to spotlights.

People

Almagro, Diego de 31 f.
Arana, Julio César 143
■ Atahualpa 27, 98 *f.*, **98**
Ayala, Felipe Huamán Poma de 38, *66*, 67
Aymará 61, 110

Ballivian, Hugo 114
Bennett, Wendell 56
Bingham, Hiram 83 f.

Llama with its proud owner.

Bitti, Bernardo 76
Bolívar, Simón 21, 92, 114 f.
Bonpland, Aimé *142*

Cadena, Maria Josefa 109
Cajamarca 20
Candía, Pedro de 17
Carvajal, Gaspar Fray de 128

Casas, Bartolomé de las 44, 136
Charles III, King 43
Charles V, King 26, 32, 44
Chavín 134
Chimú 16 f., 92, 94
Churriguera, José 28
Cobo, Bernabé 17
Columbus, Christopher 17
Creoles 28

Diez, Vaca 143
Dunlop, John Boyd *142*

Eiffel, Gustave 130

Ferdinand VI, King *61*
Fitzcarrald, Carlos Fermín 130 f.
Fujimori, Alberto *21*, 67

García, Alan 21
Garfunkel, Art 88
Gasca, Pedro de la 32
Goodyear, Charles 142
Gutierrez, Gustavo 44
Guzman, Abimal 21
Guzmán, Maria de 108

Haun, August C. 98
Holguín, Pérez de 77, 113
Huamán, Felipe 135
Huántar, Chavín de 20
Huari 20, 56
Huáscar 27, 98
Huayna Cápac 17, 27, 43, 72
Humboldt, Alexander von *142*

■ Inca 11 f., 15 ff., 22, 24, 26, 43, 50, 52 f., 60 f., **60**, 62 , 63, 68, 70 f., 74, 76, 80 ff., 85, 95, 98 f., 121, 146 f.

Kosok, Paul 103

León, Pedro Cieza de 12, 60, 67

Macheteros 132
Maldonado, Faustino 130
Mama Ocllo 52, 60, 60, 62
Manco Cápac I. 20, 52, 60, *60*, 62

Flamingo paradise: the mineral-rich lakes of the Bolivian Altiplano.

Manco Cápac II. 71, 83, 147
Mariani, Angelo 134
■ Moche 20, 23, 94, 102
Murillo, Pedro Domingo 21, 114

Nazca 16, 20
Niemann, Albert 135

Orellana, Francisco de 128

Pachacutec 60
Palma, Ricardo *66*, 67
Paniagua, Valentin 21, *21*
Paracas 16, 20
Patino, Simón Iturbi 142 f.
Paul III, Pope 43

Philip II, King 12, 34
Philip V, King 38
Pius IX, Pope 109
Pizarro, Francisco *20*, 26 f., 31 f., 43, 74, 90, 98 f., *98*
Pizarro, Gonzalo 32
Pizarro, Hernando 98
Pizarro, Pedro 99
Ponce Sanginès, Carlos 55 f.
Posnansky, Arthur 55

Recuay 20
Reiche, Maria 103
Robles, Daniel Alomia 88

San Martín, José de *20*, 21, 90
Schmid, Martin 76, 137

Simon, Paul 88
Soto, Hernando de *20*, 98
Suárez, Nicolás 143
Sucre, Antonio José de 114

Tito, Diego Quispe 77
Toledo, Alejandro *21*
Túpac Amaru I *20*, 21, 70, 74
Túpac Amaru II 70
Túpac Yupanqui 64, 67, 92

Uros 50, *50*, *53*, 54, 57

Valera, Blas 66
Vallejo, César *66*, 67
Valverde, Fray Vicente de 43

Flute player in Indígena costume.

Places, General Expressions

Floral decoration: the Calle Córdoba in the Santa Catalina Convent in Arequipa.

Handicrafts on the steps in front of the Cathedral in Arequipa.

Original headgear in Cuzco.

Weaving on the Isla Taquile.

Sometimes even the Amazon steamers need to be pushed.

Lake Titicaca sparkles deep blue in the bay off the Copacabana Peninsula, which gave its name to the world's most famous beach across the border in Brazil. The town of the same name on the peninsula is the destination of countless pilgrims every year.

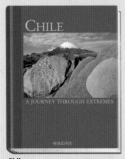
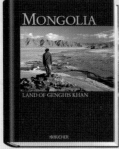

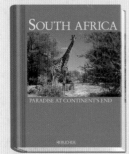
Credits and Imprint

The photographer

Arne Nicolaisen studied business management, but for some years now has compiled and presented professional slide/multivision shows of various countries. His work has featured in numerous newspapers and magazines.
www.arne-nicolaisen.de

The author

A political scientist Rainer Waterkamp also studied media sciences in Berlin. He has headed public relations for local and regional authorities as well as for the Federal Republic and frequently led photography, film and television projects. Having travelled outside Europe for many years he has written travel reports for newspapers and magazines and published travel guides and illustrated books. His book "South Africa" has already been published by C.J. Bucher Publishing. His knowledge of the Andes (Bolivia, Ecuador, Peru) is the result of various journeys undertaken since 1987, usually by jeep, and lengthier periods of residence there. He currently resides in Bonn.
Rainer.Waterkamp@t-online.de

Cover photos

Front cover: Machu Picchu (right),
Back cover: Lake Titicaca
Endpapers: Shawl.
p. 1: Girl in Chinchero,
p. 3: "Tumi" (Ceremonial knife) (above); the village elders and the mayor of Pisac on their way to Mass on Sunday (below).

Text credit

The quotation on p. 10 is taken from Mario Vargas Llosa: Death in the Andes (here in translation).

Photo credits

Ferdinand Anders, Klosterneuburg: p. 60/61; Dirk Antrop, Gent: 19 t.r., 22 b.l., 23 c.r., 144 t.l.; Archiv für Kunst und Geschichte, Berlin: p. 12, 18 b., 19 b., 20 t.r., 22 c. (3), 23 c.l., 60 b.r., 98 b. (2), 142 t. (2), 156 t.; Atlantide, Florenz: p. 8/9 (Borchi/Amantini), 28 t. and b.r., 28/29, 29, 30/31, 31 t., 32 (3), 77 l., 154/155, 155 b.r. (Borchi); Bildarchiv Preussischer Kulturbesitz, Berlin: p. 20 c.b.; corbis, Hamburg: p. 109 b.r., 147 (2); dpa, Munich: p. 21 r. (2), 67; Focus, Hamburg: p. 30 b., 33, 42, 43 t., 98 t.l., 88 b.l., 134/135 (2–8); Harald Lange/Naturbild, Bad Lausick: p. 118 b. (2); Interfoto, Munich: p. 66 t.r. (2) and b.; laif, Cologne: p. 8, 16, 24/25, 38 t., 40/41, 50 c., 60 t., 61 b., 80 b.r., 89 b., 99 t., 108 c.r., 109 r. and b.l., 119 b.l. and t.r., 146 t., 146/147, 152 t., 155 c.r., 156 t.l. and b., 128 t. (Gonzalez); Museé de l'homme, Paris: p. 23 b. (3); Okapia, Frankfurt: p. 142 t. (NAS/L. Migdale); Staatliche Münzsammlung, Munich: p. 20 t. (small photo); Hubert Stadler, Fürstenfeldbruck: p. 11 t.l., 63, 64 (2), 64/65, 70 b., 91, 92 t., 110 b., 112 t., 116/117, 126 (2), 127 r. (2), 145 b., 148/149, 152 r., 159; Süddeutscher Verlag, Munich: p. 142 c.u., 142/143, 143 (2); Ullstein Bilderdienst, Berlin: p. 142 b.l. and b.r.; Mireille Vautier, Paris: 60 l; Rainer Waterkamp, Bonn: p. 1, 3, 4 (2nd from top), 5(2) , 10 b., 20 l. and r.b.,21 l. and l. t., 28 c.l., 38b, 43 b., 52 b.l. and b.r., 64 l.t., 76 (4), 77 r., 82 l., 83 b., 84/85, 89 r.b., 103 r.t., 108 l. (2) and b.r., 108/109, 110 c. and b., 111, 112 b. (2), 113, 114 (2), 114/115, 115, 118/119, 119 b.r., 120, 120/121, 121, 122, 122/123, 124/125, 132, 133, 136 b.l. and l.t., 137 r.b., 144, 145 c.t., 146 b., 150 b., 153 (3), 154 b., 156 l. and r.c.; White Star, Florenz: p. 134 l.; Horst Welker, Filderstadt: p. 44, 45, 46, 46/47, 48/49, 152 b.

This work has been carefully researched by the author and kept up to date as well as checked by the publisher for coherence. However, the publishing house can assume no liability for the accuracy of the data contained herein.

We are always grateful for suggestions and advice. Please send your comments to:
C.J. Bucher Publishing,
Product Management
Innsbrucker Ring 15
81673 Munich, Germany
editorial@bucher-publishing.com

Translation:
Jane Michael, Munich, Germany
Proof reading: James Rumball, Hamburg, Germany
Graphic design: Werner Poll, Munich, revised by Agnes Meyer-Wilmes, Munich, Germany
Cartography:
A. Hermes, Göttingen, Germany
Product management for the German edition: Joachim Hellmuth
Product management for the English edition: Dr. Birgit Kneip
Production: Bettina Schippel
Repro: Fotolitho Longo, Bozen, Italy
Printed in Slovenia by MKT, Ljubljana

© 2008 C.J. Bucher Verlag GmbH, Munich

ISBN 978-3-7658-1715-1